Bedfordshire's

Craftsmen and Trades People

Brenda Fraser-Newstead

First published November 1995
by
The Book Castle
12 Church Street
Dunstable
Bedfordshire LU5 4RU

ISBN 1 871199 03 4

Computer typeset by Keyword, Aldbury, Hertfordshire.
Printed in Great Britain by Antony Rowe Ltd., Chippenham, Wilts.

The 'Bedfordshire's Yesteryears' oral history series is planned
to comprise:
volume 1 :   The Family, Childhood and Schooldays
volume 2 :   The Rural Scene
volume 3 :   Craftsmen and Trades People
volume 4 :   War Times and Civil Matters

Front Cover: The sweep, still bringing good luck to some.

CONTENTS

FOREWORD

I founded the International Fund for Animal Welfare twenty-six years ago to put an end to the brutal clubbing to death of baby whitecoat seals on the ice floes off the east coast of Canada. Each year since then we have been able to extend our range of activities to help protect more and more animals from man's cruelty, and from suffering in the wake of natural disasters. We have since grown to be one of the most effective organisations in the world entirely dedicated to animal welfare.

Our mission is to promote and ensure the just and kind treatment of animals; to improve the quality of their lives; to save them from extinction; and to help animals in the wake of natural disasters.

We are a non-violent organisation: we work entirely within the law, and not a penny of supporters' donations is spent on activities which might harm people in order to protect animals. We achieve results by peacefully exerting pressure for change on people, industries and even governments.

To prove our campaigns *do* work, here are examples of our recent successes, saving animals from cruelty, distress and suffering:

■ After many years of campaigning by IFAW in South Korea, a law was passed which outlaws the torturing to death of dogs and cats to 'tenderise' them for human consumption.

■ When Hurricane Andrew struck Florida, IFAW funded its action team with thousands of dollars to help co-ordinate rescue efforts with local humane societies. Hundreds of pets were kept warm, dry and well-fed until they could be reunited with their owners.

■ IFAW scientists helped lead the incredible effort to 'Save the Last Whales' by creating a massive Southern Ocean Sanctuary. Now, *one-third* of the earth's oceans are off-limits to whaling!

But we can't stop there . . . New cases of animal cruelty and suffering are being reported all the time. Canadian harp seals are once again under threat – this time they're a little older and

5

dealers in the Far East are selling their 'parts' to make aphrodisiacs and cheap leather. You may have seen TV reports about the cruel mistreatment of Asiatic Moon Bears in China, which has been exposed by IFAW.

Unless we are persistent, our good work can even be undone by industries and governments which have vested interests in the commercial exploitation of innocent animals. So, whether it's dogs, cats, seals, whales, or other animals, we cannot drop our guard, not even for a moment. We ask the public to support us and enable us to continue our lifesaving work.

For the animals.

Brian Davies, Founder, IFAW,
Warren Court, Park Road,
Crowborough, East Sussex TN6 2GA.
Tel: (01892) 663374 and 663819.

Brian Davies with seal cub.

To Omar and Yasmina

INTRODUCTION

The subject of Volume 3 in the ever-popular series of Bedfordshire's Yesteryears is craftsmen and trades people, and in writing the book I have been looking for people who have been associated with a particular craft or trade for many years, and in particular, families where several generations have been involved with the same business. Many of the skills and trades of the past may pass into extinction in this new technological age, but tradesmen existed to serve the community, and their experiences provide a unique insight into community and lifestyles in times past.

Some of the old trades described in this book have not survived, some survive in a different form, and some are being revived. This is by no means a comprehensive catalogue of the various crafts and trades which Bedfordshire has seen over the years. I regret that I personally have limited opportunities for research, as I feel that there must be many more trades people able to vividly recall their work experiences and pass on their unique recollections for our personal enrichment. Perhaps others will continue the task I have begun, but there is an urgency about gleaning the reminiscences of a passing generation, and capturing information about very different work and life experiences to those we know today.

My previous two volumes have raised an awareness of, and funds towards, research into Alzheimer's disease and for Rainbow School for children with profound and multiple 'learning difficulties'. Volume 3 is championing the cause of animal rights and welfare, and highlighting the valuable work being carried out by Brian Davies of the International Fund for Animal Welfare. I feel sure that many of my readers will support the cause of compassion towards animals on an international scale.

Brenda Fraser-Newstead

About the Author

Brenda Fraser-Newstead spent many years in the world of commerce and has been a teacher, author and examiner of Business Studies, and a company director. In recent years, however, she has forsaken that involvement and found rewarding work in social welfare and the teaching of children with special needs.

She originates from Wheathampstead in Hertfordshire, but her father was a Lutonian and she herself has lived in Bedfordshire for some twenty-five years.

Acknowledgements

The author wishes to thank, in particular, the contributors to this project, without whose help the book would not have materialised. Thanks also to the very many people, too numerous to mention personally, who have kindly given advice, assistance and support. A special word of thanks to the author's daughter, Yasmina, for her continued and valued assistance with editing and proof-reading.

Gratitude also to the following:

Mr Brian Davies,
International Fund for
Animal Welfare

Bedfordshire Social Services

Mr J Leech, Dunstable

Mr E Sabey, Bedford

Mr A Hobbs, Everton

Mr N Drury, Dunstable

Mr M T Bates, Luton

Mr P Hammond, Bedford

Mr D Stewart, Biggleswade

Mr C Bourne, Dunstable

Mr A Bayntun, Woburn

The late Mr C Horwood,
Lavendon

Staff at the Goldington Social
Centre, Barkers Lane, Bedford

Mrs Peacock, Maulden

MEN AT WORK

MEN AT WORK

Introduction

It is not such a formidable task to catalogue traditional occupations of yesteryear by comparison with the variety of occupations today. Since the onset of the industrial revolution times have changed drastically, and the mechanical has taken precedence over the hand-crafted. The personal experience of the skilled worker at his task has become an impersonal experience of man and machine. Society no longer needs trades people prepared to visit village communities: village dwellers are now mobile and able to travel out to supermarkets to obtain whatever they require. Central heating has obviated the need for the chimney sweep, the passing of the big houses with their wealthy land-owners has seen the demise of the domestic servant, the open field system of farming has seen the demise of the hedger and ditcher. However, even at the turn of the century, working patterns in Bedfordshire were largely unchanged, with sons often following fathers into crafts and occupations which their own fathers had pursued before them.

Only after the emergence of the suffragettes, and particularly the onset of the first world war, did women venture into the industrial and heavier occupations hitherto carried out by men.

The movement into the county of manufacturing companies, the coming of the railways and advances in transportation generally, demand created by the war effort, demand for manufactured goods at home and abroad, advances in education and training, and changing attitudes to women in work, all led to a greater degree of specialisation within an expanding industrialised society. The population drift from the land, and mechanisation, modern processes, rising standards of living and expectations, all these factors led to the demise of many of the old time-honoured crafts and occupations. The machine superseded the craftsman, speeded up the process, produced standard goods, and plastics replaced natural raw materials. Lifestyles have changed, and we have become de-skilled. Can we know the personal satisfaction, the pride, the thrill of applying eye and hand, knowledge and dexterity, to craft an object or complete an intricate task by hand? What happened to the 'nation of shop-keepers'? Are supermarkets denying us the pleasure of personal service and human contact? Have economic conditions and geographic mobility put an end to the family business, handed down from one generation to the next?

There is a craft revival underway, by enthusiasts anxious to preserve an important part of our heritage, and those who take pride in personal achievement. Let us learn from some of the county's remaining craftsmen and trades people through their recollections of how things used to be.

The Antiques Dealer

Pride in possession, a reverence for unique objects of the past, a fascination with the unusual, an admiration of the intricate and beautiful, a sense of living with the past, collection as investment. For all of these reasons, and many more, the antique and reproduction trades flourish. For centuries the rich have collected and decorated their homes with objects of beauty, and with antiquities, but only in comparatively recent times has the antiques trade attracted buyers from all walks of life. The Antiques Road Show and other televised programmes, along with many well-illustrated publications, has enlightened us all, kindled an interest in antiques, and aroused a desire for ownership.

'Our antiques business was started by my father, John Fennemore Sherwood, in 1923. He worked for Allens as a chargehand in the dynamo shop and had an accident when he was hit by a falling casting. There was no compensation, and he also suffered with tuberculosis, and had long periods off work. During this time he started visiting the London museums and art galleries and collected information on a variety of things. He educated himself in this business, and began doing a bit of wheeling and dealing. My mother also started selling secondhand clothes and bric-à-brac – around 1923. Times were hard then and wives often sent the old man's suit to the pawn broker! They had three children at the time. Mother went out with two suitcases full of clothes on a Saturday and would go around the villages selling clothes to farm workers, – boots, socks, waistcoats, trousers. Father was also out with his suitcases, around Cranfield area, doing the same thing. They both travelled by bus, but occasionally my mother got a lift with the gamekeepers and so on, on a pony and trap. At this time they lived at 17 Battison Street [Bedford], and my mother used the front room for the shop. They sold fireworks, bric-à-brac and anything to make a few shillings. Then they purchased a builder's shed in Battison Street, with a loft above, and went in for furniture. Things improved so they took on another shop at Great Butt Street, where County Hall stands now, and then in 1938 they moved to the premises in Prebend Street and rented it for about three or four years with the option to buy for a thousand pounds.

The shop in Prebend Street was originally a baker's shop called Town & Toll. They supplied marquees for fêtes, etc. The original 15 foot square oven is still in the back. They baked for the Kempston Barracks which was a garrison then. It was a bakery and pie shop, offering a roasting service. Next door at No. 4 was Harry Clark who was a barber. 2d a time for a haircut then, 1933. Farmers and market people in town on Saturday came for a shave and haircut. My parents still maintained the furniture shop in Battison Street and some

Sherwood's Antiques, unchanged after fifty-seven years.

years later, when the barber moved out, around 1941, they took over his shop for furniture storage. There is a photograph taken by the Bedfordshire Times, of the original shop front.

It was the depression that created my parents' business. There was both poverty and wealth in Bedford, and they catered for what the public wanted. Bedford was described in one of the colonial magazines as one of the lowest rated towns in England and colonial people who moved in, came to educate their children at the Harpur Trust Schools. These people brought with them Chinese, Oriental and African items. Since the last war, business has turned around from secondhand to antiques. Antiques have taken off in a big way only over the last twenty years or so. Twenty-five years ago I would purchase a grandfather clock for £5, but now the same thing sells at £600. Things like that have appreciated greatly in value. People are antiques-minded now, with the Road Show and magazines on the subject. At one time you could go to a house and clear it. When parents died, people couldn't afford to pay the rent, so they had to clear the house immediately. You could pick up Chinese furniture, ivory, bronze. Today they skim a place and even the rubbish goes to

Antiques, bric-a-brac, reproductions. A veritable Aladdin's Cave.

car boot sales. At one time there was no interest, just get the place cleared out so as not to pay rent and electricity.

Ashburnham and Shakespeare Roads, among others, were areas of affluence, with large houses employing butlers, servants, maids and so on, but now they have all gone and the houses are converted to flats. Many of these original owners were service people, colonial people, who brought a great many objects into Bedford from all over the world. There was a terrific amount of Oriental stuff, Indian, Japanese, at one time.

Both of my parents worked in this business. I have always been involved, but actually took over in 1970, when my father was still working here. My mother died about 1967 and he died ten years later. He had suffered with his lungs as a result of having TB, and actually lived with me for the last four years of his life. He was born at Bradwell near Wolverton and was originally a blacksmith engineer with the railway, before working for Allens.

When mother and father ran the business, many people had fallen on hard times and the most surprising people would turn up anxious to sell off possessions. The Bowes Lyons used to bring things here for sale, Lydia, the Duchess of Bedford, the Marquess's mother, would come to buy things. She would deal with my mother and would have a cup of tea with mother. She was a lovely person. I used to have to take a cup of tea out to her chauffeur! We had film directors. Miss Hodgeson was a top antiques dealer in London then, and she used to bring all these people down. They all came to buy. She would recommend what they should buy. During the war we had the American pilots. They even wanted to buy the door here and take it back to the States, because it contains stained glass panels. There was a lot of stuff coming out of London – china and tea sets and quality stuff, much of which was shipped to the States. Prisoners of war made items out of tin, bone, etc. and mother used to buy from them. Some came from Italy and elsewhere and mother would send a parcel to their home instead of giving them money. Money boxes, cigarette/lighter cases, metal planes, tanks, decorative boxes. They had to wear big patches to show they were prisoners of war, but many worked on the farms around Bedford. They were pushed into the war, like many other people. They were nice people.

I started repairing watches before the last war, old pocket watches and clocks. My father didn't do that. I've had thirty-six years in engineering, at the Igranic. I also restore barometers. The most intricate clock I ever restored was like a castle on a plynth, under a glass dome. The drawbridge came down, doors opened and a row of people came out, horses, men and dogs, and paraded around. The windmill turned and the watermill, and a music box played. This was the most intricate piece I have ever worked on. It was probably German. Courtiers, followers, with pikes, in procession. They came out on a sort of paper ribbon, and this happened every hour. My father sold it to an antiques dealer in Luton.

At one time you bought and sold quickly to get a quick

A caravan similar to the one used by Mrs Sherwood, except that hers had iron-shod wooden wheels placed outside the van.

turnover. Now you can get social security. My father applied once and was offered a shilling! You needed to make a quick profit. My parents had five children and made a reasonable living, and a bit of profit. In later years things got better and they bought a bungalow at Snettisham near King's Lynn, for holidays. The bungalow was lost when the high tide disaster struck the east coast some years ago, when many of our neighbours there lost their lives. Later they bought a twenty foot section of ground on the Wilstead Road and then two sections afterwards. There was an old man lived in a caravan, called Warren. He kept rabbits and was a wirey old man. The ground belonged to him. He had a cup of Oxo and a slice of bread about three times a day, and this was how he lived. That would have been about 1950. Mother bought an old caravan which was used for road repairs, and which contained a bunk and a stove. She put it on the ground and when they closed, she would go over there and have a cup of tea. She'd planted out a little garden, and it was quite a nice place. Willy Warren came over to have tea and cakes with her. He always put his best suit on for the occasion, and sat bolt upright. To have tea with Mrs Sherwood was a big day out for him. He was about eighty then. He had never been to the seaside and it was arranged that he would accompany my mother on a trip to the bungalow at the seaside. He was to bike over to Bedford with his suitcase and join us on our trip by taxi. He never turned up, and the police eventually found him dead by his bike. He had suffered a heart attack. They never did find his case of money. After that, mother cancelled her trip to Hunstanton, and she eventually bought his plot of ground at Wilstead.'

PERCIVAL 'GEOFF' SHERWOOD

The Apprentice

Apprenticeships were a means of training young school leavers in an economical and efficient manner. Young people would be legally bound to an employer, for a stated period of time, often four or five years, during which time the trainee (the 'apprentice') would earn a small wage, in return for the opportunity to work alongside a skilled craftsman or a skilled labour force, often with attendance at college on a 'day-release' basis, in order to study the theoretical aspects of the trade.

The apprentice would emulate the work practices of his seniors, and learn from their instruction and by observation, over a long period of time. From this experience he would develop skills and attitudes and at the end of his term of apprenticeship would be free to leave, or – as was more usual – would be engaged as an employee.

In return for his efforts, and for the provision of tools of the trade, (and in some trades – printing, for example – the apprentice lived on the premises), the employer would expect loyalty and industry, the apprentice commencing by undertaking rather more menial and repetitive tasks, and finally acquiring the status of craftsman. Upon completion of his training, the apprentice would produce, for example, an item of furniture, which would give testament to his ability and standard of workmanship.

Whether formal or informal, the system of apprenticeship guaranteed that standards in the industry or trade would be maintained, and all the knowledge and skills acquired over the years would be transmitted to the next generation.

'My father he 'ad me apprenticed at Luton at Clark's Machine Tool Company. I 'ad to get there at six o'clock in the morning so I 'ad to leave Dunstable at 5.30 on a pushbike, and if you was after two minutes past six you was shut out for the day, and that's true and if you lost so many quarters as they called 'em in a week, then they paid you nothing whatsoever. I only got five bob a week, that weren't much, and they were very busy and we 'ad to work overtime.

We started six in the morning 'til half past eight to nine breakfast: nine o'clock to one then dinner, one to two, and two 'til half past five, then from half past five 'til nine o'clock, overtime that was. Overtime for us apprentices wa'nt above a penny or three 'a-pence. But any rate we 'ad to do it and if you asked the foreman for a night off do you know what he used to say "You're a lazy b..." he says, "you're too lazy to do anything". But there was no doubt about it, that was the way to bring 'em up, that was. I tell you, that 'ardened 'em up and made people realise and thankful, diff'rent to what they are now. Well, I don't know, the hours they work now, I'm sure. If we did want a night off they used to carry on alarming. It's true, we got done at one o'clock on a Saturday.

If you was two minutes late the man used to shut the gates. He loved it too. It didn't matter how you argued. "I'm not allowed to let you in", he said, "time's time". But I tell you what, I honestly think it does boys good, because now they're pampered – they get more money now while they're at school than I used to get when I was at work.

After I was out of my time, I got a good job really at SKF Co

Tool, and SKF at that time of the day were the best paying firm in the district. My wages then were £4.10s a week but I used to 'ave to start at eight o'clock, work overtime every night, overtime 'til eight o'clock and you got orf at five o'clock on a Friday and then we used to work 'til one o'clock on a Saturday. But o' course there was no Income Tax whatsoever. And another thing at that time o' the day you could buy a jolly good suit for £2, you could. As a matter of fact a cheaper suit you could buy for thirty-five shillings and then the fifty shilling tailors came about. But as I say you could get a jolly good suit – a navy blue, and you can't get a navy blue today 'cos nobody will guarantee the dye but years ago they used to guarantee it and that was fifty shillings at that, hand made. Things were very very cheap.'

ERIC THORNE

An Indenture of Apprenticeship.

THIS INDENTURE WITNESSETH That George Fisher of the age of Fifteen years on the twentysixth day of October last by and with the consent of his Mother Mary Fisher of Maulden in the County of Bedford Widow and with the approval and concurrence of His Grace The Most Noble Frances Charles Hastings Duke of Bedford KG of Woburn Abbey Woburn in the said County of Bedford Robert Read Veterinary Trade . . . . ., The Reverend Henry Cobbe, Clerk (Rector of Maulden) George Street, Farmer, William Butt, Farmer, James Brightman, Farmer, Arthur Hallworth, Farmer and George Young, Butcher, all now or late of Maulden aforesaid and John James Adkins of Tingrith in the said County, Farmer, Trustees (inter alia) of Robert Becketts Maulden Apprentice Fund, testified by their executing these presents Doth put himself Apprentice to

William Thomas Sharpe, of Ampthill, in the said County, Plumber and Glazier to learn his Art and with him after the manner of an Apprentice to serve until the twentysixth day of October, one thousand eight hundred and ninety three, During which term the said Apprentice his master faithfully shall serve, his secrets keep, his lawful commands everywhere gladly do, he shall do no damage to his said Master nor see it done by others but to his power shall tell or forthwith give warning to his said Master nor lend them unlawfully to any he shall not commit fornication nor contract matrimony within the said term he shall not play at Cards, dice Tables or any other unlawful games whereby his said Master may have any loss with his own goods or others during the said term without the license of his said Master he shall neither keep nor sell, he shall not haunt taverns or playhouses nor absent himself from his Master's service unlawfully but in all things as a faithful apprentice he shall behave himself towards his said Master and all his during the said term and the said William Thomas Sharpe in consideration of the good and faithful services to be performed by his said apprentice and in consideration of the sum of Ten Pounds paid by the said Trustees out of the said Apprentice Fund upon the execution of these presents the receipt whereof he the said William Thomas Sharpe doth hereby acknowledge and of the Board Lodging Washing and necessaries to be found and provided for the said Apprentice by the said Mary Fisher as hereinafter mentioned Doth hereby for himself his executors and administrators Covenant with the said Trustees and the survivors or survivor of them that he the said William Thomas Sharpe his executors and administrators and assigns his said Apprentice in the Art of a Plumber and glazier which he useth by the best means that he can shall teach and instruct or cause to be taught and instructed finding for his said Apprentice proper working tools (except a Diamond) and also payments the said Mary Fisher or to or for the use of the said Apprentice the weekly wages following three shillings per week up to the twentysixth day of October next such weekly payments to increase one shilling each succeeding year up to the twentysixth day of October one thousand eight hundred and ninetyfive and nine shillings per week during the last year of the said term

AND IT IS HEREBY DECLARED by and between the said parties hereto that in case of sickness of the part of the said Apprentice the said weekly wages hereby reserved are to cease for so long a time as the said Apprentice shall be unable to fulfil the duties imposed on him under and by virtue of this Indenture And the said Mary Fisher for the consideration aforesaid and of the weekly payments so to be made to her as aforesaid Doth Covenant and agree to and with the said

William Thomas Sharpe and to and with the said Trustees and the survivors or survivor of them that during the whole of the term aforesaid she will find and provide for her said son good and sufficient meat, drink, lodging, clothes, washing and all other necessaries that may be required for him And for the true performance of the Covenants and Agreements aforesaid all and either of the said parties bindeth himself herself and themselves unto the other or others of them to these presents IN WITNESS whereof the said parties to these presents have hereunto set their hands and seals the sixteenth day of August in the year of our LORD, one thousand eight hundred and eightyeight.

George Fisher
Mary Fisher
(her mark)
William Thomas Sharpe

Henry Cobbe
George Stacey
William Butt

Signed sealed and schrivened by the said George Fisher Mary Fisher William Thomas Sharpe Henry Cobbe George Street and William Butt in the presence of RM White, Clerk to Mrs Tanqueray, Solicitor Ampthill Beds.

The Baker

Gone are the days when bread, cakes and pastries were baked by the local baker, and when the baker did his rounds, selling bread from the cart or van. Jam doughnuts, jam tarts, jam turnovers, Eccles, rock cakes, gingerbread, bread pudding, custard tarts, iced buns, cream buns, chocolate eclairs, fairy cakes. No boxed cakes, no pre-sliced and wrapped bread taken from a supermarket shelf, but good wholesome food fresh from the bakery, with bread often still warm from baking. Christmas cakes and Sunday joints could be left with the baker for cooking, for just a few pence.

Each baker knew his customers personally, and his reputation and livelihood depended upon the quality of the product he sold.

William Juffs, Wootton Baker and Mealman, 1912

'I left school at twelve, as the Great War was underway and the children were allowed to leave early, providing they had a job to go to, which I had. My employer was Mr William Juffs, who was one of the three local bakers [in Wootton], the others being Mr Keep and Mr Fardell. The bakehouse was a part of the Juffs family's sixteenth century home. I almost lived with the Juffs when I left school, and often had my meals with them. In addition to baking, Mr Juffs kept livestock including pigs and cows, and horses for the delivery rounds. It was a thriving business, run by William Juffs and his father, Henry – "Pa Juffs" – who came from Houghton Conquest and was in business as baker and mealman, selling feed stuff such as bran, corn and so on. I sold all these things around the village and there was always a demand, as everyone in Wootton kept hens, pigs and rabbits. I also bought and sold at markets in St. Neots and Bedford, and I reckon I have bought

William Juffs' bakery in Wootton. Left – right: Henry, Bill's grandfather, Aunt Elsie, and the young Fred Burraway.

hundreds of hens and rabbits in my time.

The Juffs' home and bakery was a hive of activity. The cottage was home to William Juffs, his wife and son, his mother and father and also two sisters, Elsie and Kit. Henry retired from the bakery business in 1936 and went to live in Church Road. His hobby was pigeon racing and this was a hobby he pursued throughout his life. In fact, it was a popular hobby with many people at that time. He died in 1940.

My first job was milking cows. I had to bring them in for milking each morning and I can remember running like hell at 5 o'clock across the dark fields to round 'em up. After milking them, I'd take the milk to Northerns, who sent it away with his own milk. Northerns lived at Great Brook, the big local farm. The old man used a cultivator, which I used to help him with at times. Then the cows had to be cleaned out – there was a muck yard by the bakery, and the muck was sold as manure and fetched away in cart loads.

Having learned the trade, I spent all my working life at the bakery, working for this family, until my retirement. I'd make up a batch of dough in the dough trough, using a sack of flour, fifteen gallons of water, salt and yeast. It all had to be mixed up and left to "prove". The oven held 250 loaves and we filled it two or three times a day. The oven had to be set, and the coal fire stoked up. The furnace was filled about twice and then you knew when it was hot enough. We would throw in some flour and if it burnt quickly you knew it was ready. We used to make fruit cakes up on a Thursday, round ones and long ones, and these all sold. I'd do anything at the bakery including feeding the horses and deliveries off the cart. I learned my baking from Pa Juffs. People used to bring turkeys, geese and hens to us at Christmas, for roasting. We'd put less coal on for these and gauge the heat carefully. We used a smaller fire for lower temperature cooking, what we called a "fair heat".

I've lived in Wootton all my life. Years ago I knew everyone in the Wootton area. It was all very quiet then. I used to go round Marston, Pillinge and Broadmead, Bourne End and Wootton delivering. On Good Fridays we made thousands of Hot Cross Buns and delivered them, also at the big houses – Wootton House and the vicarage. Ethel Pearce was the cook there, but she didn't make the bread. People had fresh bread delivered every day and paid nothing for the delivery. Apart from the three village bakers, there was also one at Marston, Harry Lovell, and Mr Pulley from Cranfield.

Bakers were exempt from call-up so I didn't serve in the forces during the second world war. During the war the village didn't go short of bread, even though there was rationing. There was plenty of flour to be had.

I was at the bakehouse the day William's son was born – Bill they call him. William gave me ten shillings that day. He was so happy! That was a lot of money then.

I got married when I was twenty-two and took a cottage for half a crown a week near the bakehouse. I've brought up six

children and I've never been hard up in all my life. My son
Ray still works for Bill Juffs. William Juffs retired at the age
of 65; Bill was more enthusiastic about horses than baking
and so the business was taken over by Mr Howitt for a few
years. When he gave it up, I retired. Then Bill established his
riding school.
   Even after I retired I used to get requests for cakes,
gingerbread and so on.'

FREDERICK BURRAWAY

The Blacksmith and Farrier

Up to the time of the first war, blacksmiths were always in
great demand and the forge was a common sight in every
village. The shoeing of horses – working horses, farm horses,
riding horses – maintaining carriages, traps and gigs. The
repair of farm implements and equipment, the making of
horseshoes, ploughs, farm gates, hinges, ornamental garden
gates, lamp brackets, harrows, hurdles and so on. Repairing
pots and pans, chain-making, tool-making. The smithy was
never out of work.

There were five blacksmiths operating in Bedford in the
period between the wars, but time saw the gradual demise of
the horse, and only one of the Bedford blacksmiths survived –
the one which mechanised and travelled to the customer to
shoe on site.

'I left school at thirteen and started work as a blacksmith at
the Blacksmith's Shop in Dane Street, Bedford, in the days
when blacksmiths were always in great demand. There were
the gentry's carriages and riding horses to be kept in order
and shod, the farmers' traps and gigs, the farm horses, and
carriers and tradesmen's horses to shoe. There were the
"railways horses" which were owned by the railway and were
stabled in Ashburnham Road opposite Midland Station. They
delivered around town to shops and factories, goods which
had arrived by rail. They pulled trolleys. Eventually they

29

The blacksmith's in Dane Street. Ted with a horse belonging to Stopsley's of Clapham, and 'a difficult horse to shoe'.

Dobbin, last of the railway horses in Bedford.

were replaced by mechanised vehicles and were auctioned off at The Elephant and Castle in London, – all except one called Dobbin, who was sold to Miss Lawrence of Wilstead, who had stables at the bottom of Cotton End Hill. She cared for Dobbin in his retirement.

The smithy was never out of work. There were then five blacksmiths in Bedford and I am proud to say that I was the only one of the Bedford blacksmiths to survive. This is because I decided to mechanise so that I could travel to my customers and shoe on site.

My starting wage at the Blacksmith's Shop was nine shillings per week and I worked from 6am to 5pm. Breakfast was 8 or 9am and dinner from 1 to 2pm. I quickly learned the trade and by the age of fifteen I was making the shoes and shoeing horses myself. One Saturday, when I was paid, I remember asking for a rise. I was given one shilling extra and told "think yourself lucky".

Ted's smithy in Russell Street, Bedford, over sixty years ago.

By the age of sixteen I had passed all my examinations, and I won my first prize for shoeing in 1926. I went on to win others. I married when I was twenty-three and moved to 58 Russell Street where I worked as a blacksmith until 1970. I was my own master for thirty years, during which time I also made cartwheels and employed a wheelwright. Between us we produced trolleys. I later learnt to drive and bought my own van, in which I travelled around to my customers to shoe their horses – every one was shod hot.

My working day often began at 4am during the winter, when I would go to Charles Franklin's in Cauldwell Street to put the screws in twenty-one horses so they could go out if the roads were rough. This meant tapping a hole into the shoe and fitting screws so the horses didn't slip on the icy roads. This work had to be finished by 8am when the horses were taken out on their coal deliveries.

My mobile round began with a stop at Mr Murdoch's, Corporation Farm, Cardington, then at Tommy Monk's, The Maltings, Southill Road, Cardington, Mr Finlay, Lake's Farm, Cardington, Mr Mayes, Middle Farm, Cople, Mr Juffs Riding School, Wootton, Tinsley's Riding School, Clapham. On Saturdays and Sundays Johnson's High Street Bedford, Harry Sell, Fish Shop, Silver Street. Harry had some really good ponies. He wore a straw hat and white coat (and this is going back forty or fifty years), took his fish around town on the cart. He was a smart character, wore a white handkerchief in his top pocket. He was meticulously clean and would lift up the pony's collar to check for dust and if he found any he would send it back for cleaning. Canvin's in Harpur Street followed. They had five horses and delivered meat by horse and cart. Then Briant's in Silver Street, and Hoppers Corn Mill. Next came Miss Armsden at the butcher's shop next to the Empire.

I allowed myself one hour to shoe a horse and got two shod before breakfast, two or three before dinner and three more in the afternoon. The charge was five shillings per pony and the

Ted, the mobile blacksmith, by the hay barn.

shoes generally lasted three or four weeks. I believe the cost is now ten pounds per animal. Shoes could be salvaged from the shire horses and re-made for ponies.

I have also shod for gypsies, and they were the best payers. They called on a Saturday and would usually say "put some thick 'ns on", then they would give me another shilling. They would camp anywhere, and brought their horses in to market. I still remember their caravans and the lovely copper they had. I always found them to be fair and generous.

I started buying and selling horses when I was about thirty-five, on my rounds. I used to have a pony and trap for my work then, and finished up with a Land Rover and horse box. I have entered horses for the Horse of the Year Show and Wembley, and have travelled all over the country showing horses, including Chalfont St. Peters, where all the riding schools had their annual Shows. Twice I qualified for Wembley, in two consecutive years. On each occasion I would be sitting in the audience in the front line. My best horse "Pendley Carnaby" I bought for one hundred and fifty pounds

Pendley Carnaby, ridden by Maria Eros, Ted's niece.

about fifteen years ago at two-and-a-half years old. I schooled him on and eventually sold him to a buyer in Jersey for one thousand pounds. My niece rode my horses at the shows and I taught her how to shoe. She still works with horses, on a local stud farm.

Horses have been my life. There was one occasion when I was kicked by a horse and fractured my ankle and broke my leg, after which I was twenty-one weeks in plaster, but this didn't dampen my enthusiasm for horses.

I went to school with children of horse dealers – James Smith, 21 Conquest Road. There were fifteen children in this family and I learned a great deal from them about horses. There are a lot of tricks to learn in the horse trade, and I got most of my knowledge from these friends of mine. I went to school with their children and went around with them after leaving school. I have never needed a horse doctor, as my dealer friends taught me how to treat sick animals. "Strangles" can be dealt with by rubbing the throat with white oils, and

hot beers and ginger can be used for "pink eyes".
    *Both of my parents died when I was sixteen, my father of
cancer and my mother of a heart attack. I was forced to stand
on my own two feet and to take care of my younger brother
and sister. Life wasn't easy, and it was difficult to make ends
meet, when the rent was six shillings a week.*
    *I have shoed for many traders, farmers and other notables,
including Colonel Rushed near Olney, Lord and Lady
Denham of Bozeat, Earl Beatty, Chicheley Hall (he was fifty
and had a wife of nineteen!), the Oakley Hunt and Milton
Kennels, farmers at Stagsden, Mr Frossell and Harry
Newman and his brother George.'*

EDWARD (TED) PAGE

The Bonnet Maker and Straw Trade

South Bedfordshire became an important centre for straw
plait manufacture because of the suitability of its fine wheat
straw and also as a result of the silica within the straw which
provided strength without brittleness. Straw bonnets and
hats date from the eighteenth century and until about 1870
most of the plait was made in the counties of Bedfordshire,
Hertfordshire, Essex and Buckinghamshire. In the early
1800s a Dunstable blacksmith invented an instrument for
splitting straws which enabled the workers to introduce a
host of different designs and patterns, much lighter in weight
than whole straw plait.

    In 1870 plait from China became imported into Britain.
The plait from China was much cheaper and better than the
commoner sort of home-made plaits: hat making from the
new plaits increased and many of the younger plaiters
learned the art of sewing the China plait into hats and
bonnets.

    The introduction of the sewing machine revolutionised the
trade, production increased greatly and for Luton the story
was one of continued progress. The population doubled
within thirty years.

Mr Edmund Wiseman, AMIME, whose inventions revolutionised the straw hat trade. Mr Wiseman of Luton, produced his Rapid Concealed-Stitch machine (Luton's greatest invention), making possible firmer work than that sewn by hand.
Photo: Pub T G Hobbs, Luton and Neighbourhood Illustrated.

From 1891 Japanese plaits were imported. From Italy came Tuscans, Pedals, and Chips in many forms. From Switzerland came braids, plaits and trimmings made from straw, chip, hemp, hair. etc. Because of the unlimited supply of foreign plait Luton became a firm leader in the hat industry. Even King Edward and Queen Alexandra purchased hats of Bedfordshire-made plait.

Materials used were not just straw: in some seasons the materials used could be made of wood (called chip plait), from grasses and rushes, from cotton and silk, horsehair, mohair, palm leaf, chiffon, lace, and even paper. Also important, was felt particularly in the late summer and autumn months. Thousands of dozens of velvet and 'ready-to-wear' hats were produced for markets all over the world, in great variety.

Mr E W Hart's bleaching, dyeing and felt-body works.
Photo: Pub T G Hobbs, Luton and Neighbourhood Illustrated.

An early morning scene in Oxford Road, Luton.
Photo: Pub T G Hobbs, Luton and Neighbourhood Illustrated.

Luton's bleaching and dyeing was the best in the world, largely due to the chemical constitution of the water and applied scientific methods. With the discovering of aniline dyes, mauve or Perkins' violet colours were patented in 1856. Then came Hoffman red (magenta or rosaniline). Aniline dyes gave a brilliant and fast colour. Over three hundred different shades were often produced in one day.

Luton became served by three railway companies, from which both the hat industry and the railways flourished.

Sewing machines made a great contribution to the industry. American steam driven machines were used in the early attempts to mechanise production and at a later date domestic sewing machines were modified to accommodate the production of hats. In June 1878 Mr Edmund Wiseman, a Lutonian, patented a machine specially for sewing straw hats and bonnets. This concealed stitch machine became world-famous. The invention of blocking machines also

George Street, Luton. A common scene with cartloads of returned empties plying the street.
Photo: Pub T G Hobbs, Luton and Neighbourhood Illustrated.

brought about advances in manufacture, as pressing by this method gave precision, both to the edge of the crown and the division of the brim. Hat presses then came into being.

Over the past decade, hats have again been popularised by Princess Diana, and Luton still leads the field in the production of fashionable headwear.

The Bonnet Maker

'My father was a bonnet maker, according to his marriage certificate, and worked for Robinson & Butt, 38/40 Bute Street, Luton. The boss had been a factory worker himself, in the hat trade, but left to start up on his own, and my father went with him. At the outbreak of the first world war father was too old for the army and continued to work for Robinson & Butt. I later worked for the same firm and on one occasion was given my dad's wages by mistake. It was a shock – I never knew he earned money like that, but then he was as good as three men.

I left school on 2 April 1914. My father got me into an iron moulding foundry to learn the trade, and this is where I began work. The war broke out shortly afterwards and I left work to sign up but was not passed because of my eyes, so then I was out of work and took a job in the hat factory. I could make a hat when I was about thirteen but only as amusement, not to earn money. I had been at work to watch father, whilst still at school. When you do it all day it plays with your hands because you work in steam. Until your hands get hardened you are blistered but eventually they toughen up. For the first twelve months the governor wouldn't let me touch a white hat because I'd dirty it. Once your hands have got set they never sweat again. It's very strange.

There are two seasons for hats, straw hats and felt hats. There is an enormous range of plait to make straw hats: Hampton, Neboka, Liserie, Pampas Grass, Pedal, Tagel. These are all different plaits, different widths – and Birds Eye is just like the eye of a bird, very tiny, one of the smallest

Frank Chapman with his in-laws, Mr and Mrs William Rowe and family, of 13 Buxton Road, Luton, in the summer of 1925.
Left to right, rear: William Rowe, Frank, Horace Rowe, Cyril Rowe and Stanley Rowe. Left to right, front: Florence and William Rowe, Sarah, William's mother, Lilian (Frank's wife), Derrick (Frank's son).

plaits from China and Japan. Some plait was grown locally. In the villages around here the women, when they cut out corn, used to get the stalks and they had an instrument which ripped open the straw to make three to seven pedals, all different thicknesses. Our straw in Bedfordshire was very suitable.

When the season was finished there was about six weeks with nothing doing. Men had to go on the Labour. Me, with a large family, was smart enough to make myself almost indispensable. I never went piecework but drew wages for fifty-two weeks of the year, which was what I wanted. These fellows earned big money but on Fridays they went pub crawling, all of them, and when I met them in the town they would say "Lend us half a crown", "Have you got a Woodbine

Mr G W Gilder's straw hat show rooms.
Photo: Pub T G Hobbs, Luton and Neighbourhood Illustrated.

*to give us?" The designer and her sister would be there during
the slack periods and I was there in case I was wanted. Some
days I never saw a soul, there was just the man who locked up
and looked after the boiler and the heating. There was always
a gap between felts and straws or straws and felts. The buyers
have a tidy-up I suppose. On a certain day they stopped
buying, twice a year.*

*The straw hats were for children and ladies, mainly
ladies. We didn't do men's boaters in our factory, Robinson &
Butt. Felt hats were dyed and ostrich feathers used in one
period, lots of feathers. There were about a dozen private
houses where they curled feathers. There would be a sign
outside "Feathers Dyed and Curled". Ostrich was the most
popular. Hoods were made of felt, but some were velours with
a nap on. Another was beaver, a very long nap. They were
decorated with fur, melazine. There was a big variety of
materials for decoration, including furs. I paid 6/6d for my*

boaters when I was young. You could loosen the leather for a perfect fit. The first time I went out with my wife she sat on my boater!

In the old days, instead of a lining like they have ribbon today, they used to be made of leather, but in the cheap hats they used ordinary tissue paper. The designer took patterns from a Kaleidoscope and made a mount of these things to trim the hats. The hats were all bleached and dyed, by a specialist firm. Hypo and Sorrell were used for bleaching. It had a very pungent smell, difficult to describe. When my lad was about fourteen I couldn't afford to send him to a Higher Grade school but there was an examination in Luton and the subject was Lyles Sugar. He thought they said Lyles the bleachers and dyers and wrote an essay on bleaching and dyeing and made such a good job of it that he won a free pass to Luton Modern, which was in Park Square. You had to pay there, but he got a free place.

I worked there about thirty-nine years until the governor died. The business was sold then, to a manufacturer's son who had just come out of the army, after the Second World War. He made a mess of it and we had the bailiffs in. My eldest son worked at Electrolux. He was in Care and Quality. I was fifty-five and a half when he had the bailiffs in and my son didn't know whether I was any good at my job but thought I would be out of work. He said I could come and work for him but I pointed out that in nine and a half years I was due to retire, and felt they wouldn't employ me at fifty-five. Anyway, I thought it over and thought it would be a nice change, nothing to lose, and I would be sure of my money, so I decided to have a go and joined him as an Inspector. I'd been an Inspector in the hat trade, used to correcting any faults with the hats.'

FRANK CHAPMAN

Mr Stephen Sapwell's warehouse and blocking room.
Photo: Pub T G Hobbs, Luton and Neighbourhood Illustrated.

Messrs Dillingham's Straw hat factory.
Photo: Pub T G Hobbs, Luton and Neighbourhood Illustrated.

Messrs T Lyle & Sons' straw plait bleach and dye works.
Photo: Pub T G Hobbs, Luton and Neighbourhood Illustrated.

Messrs J & G Squires' straw and felt hat showroom.
Photo: Pub T G Hobbs, Luton and Neighbourhood Illustrated.

Mr C H Osborne's dye works and hat factory in Melson Street.
Photo: Pub T G Hobbs, Luton and Neighbourhood Illustrated.

A view of Mr J Ellis's straw plait and felt-body dye works.
Photo: Pub T G Hobbs, Luton and Neighbourhood Illustrated.

The Brickmaker

Until roughly the mid-nineteenth century, when rail transportation facilitated the movement of bricks around the country, it was common for bricks to be made locally, where the raw materials existed. Most villages had at least one brickmaker who would produce bricks, tiles and pipes. Although bricks have been used locally since the fifteenth century, cottages were frequently constructed not of brick, but stone, timber and wattle and daub, and of flint. The brickmaker catered for local needs, and large-scale brickmaking has occurred as a result of improved transportation, government policy and widespread demand. The most important producer of bricks locally is the London Brick Company in Stewartby.

'In my younger days the main place for work in this area was the brickworks. You had to wait your turn to get in there.

Stan's father (centre right) and two uncles (centre row) at the Brickworks before the first world war.

Several men from the village biked to Bedford to Allens but it was rare for men to go to Bedford to work. Most men walked to the brickworks, but quite a number had cycles.

It was a job to get work on a farm too, at that time. I used to work on the farm in the summer before leaving school but I discovered that the brickworks paid better money. Thirty shillings a week was the farm labourer's wage, and for a forty-eight hour week. We boys got sixteen shillings a week.

I left school at fourteen. There was no chance to get anywhere else no matter how clever you were, unless you were a farmer's son and could go to the Bedford Modern. Parents had to send their children out to work because they were not as well off as we are now.

It was customary in those days for every village to have its own brickworks. There were three in Wootton, one was at Keeley Corner, where the clay was dug up by hand. Tinkers Corner was another site, but this finished when I was a boy. I remember the moulds in the sheds for making the bricks and tiles and there was a kiln. There was also a brickworks in Fields Road. The clay was dug from the pit from where we got our water. This belonged to Jim Somerfield and his son. I remember them making tiles and pipes and delivering them by horse and cart. Farmers used the pipes then. There were not too many thatched cottages in Wootton. Hand-made bricks were made at Marston from about 1860 and this was still going on after I got married in 1935. It finished when the second world war started. It belonged to Franklins the coal people at Bedford.

I started work on 10 March. First year I went I walked from Wootton to Wootton Pillinge. The company belonged to B J Forder at that time. There were originally two brickworks, before I started, one called Kimberley and the other Klondyke, started about 1899 about the time of the gold mining in South Africa. When I started it wasn't a big place. Forder had bought the Kimberley yard and used to transport bricks from the Klondyke yard to Kimberley by pony, using a little railway. At Kimberley they used to make tiles and pipes with the yellow clay which is thrown away now, called the "gault gold". These were moulded, sanded and put on racks to dry, – dried over pipes that is, and then kilned, – burnt in the kiln. They're now extruding bricks, and using Oxford clay. It is about twenty feet down.

I worked at the brick works for fifty-one years, and did most jobs in production, eventually becoming Production Foreman, a job which I held for twenty-nine years or so.

What revolutionised the brick industry was the lift trucks and conveyor belt. They have miles and miles of these. At one time there was an endless chain, it was pulled out of the "knot hole" with waggons. There used to be a knot hole for Kimberley but this has since been filled in. Fellows used to go bathing in it. The navvy (used for digging the clay) would just go through the knot hole.

The brickworks at Stewartby, then known as Wootton Pillinge, were started in 1899 and only contained nine small kilns. Then in 1927-28 it started to expand, (under the Housing Acts of 1919, 1923 and 1926 the government provided subsidies for builders, which led to a boom in the industry) and the kilns were made bigger. I was about twenty then. Around 1930 they started to build more kilns, and the works grew. Eighteen million bricks were made one week, which was the record make.

Stewartby took its name from the Stewart family who, with the Keeble brothers, took over Forder's business interests when he retired. Percy Malcolm Stewart, Managing Director and later Chairman, was knighted in 1937 for his services to the industry. It was he who began in 1926 to develop his model village. He is said to have been a generation ahead of his time in management/labour relations, having introduced welfare and pension schemes, death and disablement benefits, joint consultation, profit-sharing, and holidays with pay. Strikes and stoppages were almost unknown during his time at the brickworks. Sir Malcolm retired in 1950, having been

Stewartby in the 'thirties, photographed by Stan using his Box Camera, still in pristine condition.

Chairman of London Brick for twenty-five years.

At one time, during the first world war, the engineering section of the company engaged in munitions work, producing explosive shells, and high explosives, which were stored in disused kilns, closed because of the trade recession.'

STANLEY LOVELL

My father worked as a Setter for the London Brick Company, then known as Forders Ltd. His job was to set the green bricks in the chambers. He later became a burner. About twenty men and as many boys, or young men, from Wootton, would walk together across the fields over the Woburn Road and down to London Brick, and work from six in the morning until six in the evening. This was before the time of the bicycle, or before they were affordable. I was about ten or eleven when I had my first bike.'

FREDERICK BURRAWAY

The Carrier

Until regular bus services connected villages and towns, and village to village, the carrier was the poor man's mode of transport. Something of an intermediary between taxi and bus, as operated today, the carrier plied his way between certain points at given times each week, visiting particular places en route. The carrier might visit a village in the morning, and return during the afternoon, and in addition to carrying passengers, might collect or deliver goods by arrangement. Often the starting point was the local inn, and prospective passengers could book a collection point and time, so that the carrier would call to pick them up as he departed. Closed carriages or open carriages, or the humble pony and trap, the journey gave passengers time to chat and to pass on the local news and gossip. A leisurely ride, views to enjoy, and acquaintances to renew.

'During 1922 we were back again in Thurleigh, this time to thatch the roof of a smallholder's cottage and it was here that romance with the farmer's daughter and myself began. At the time she was only seventeen years of age and being the only child, her parents thought the world of her. Apart from the farming, her parents ran a carrier's business and also a small village store.

From this time onwards, most of my spare time was spent helping her parents on the agricultural side. On Saturdays, her father and mother would drive the carrier's van on its usual weekly trip to Bedford, picking up passengers on the way, usually about ten or twelve people. One can well imagine the amount of tongue wagging and exchange of gossip and news which took place on both journeys! Most villages at that time had their own horse-drawn carrier's vans and on Saturdays they could be seen making their way to the town. All this slowly disappeared with the arrival of the motor bus. The "Old George", a well-known public house and hostelry in town was where the horses and van were "put up". It was here that parcels and goods from some of the leading shops and stores would be loaded on to the van, to be delivered to various places en route home. At that time, quite a few people living in the country made their own bread and it was not an unusual sight to see half a dozen cans tied to the axle underneath the van filled with brewers yeast, to be used for bread making. With the jolting and swinging of the cans, the yeast would start to "work", therefore lifting the lids from the cans, thus losing some of the contents.

As the return of the van was expected, one would stand and listen for the clip-clop of the horses, and the rumbling of the van in the distance. Some of the husbands would meet their wives and help to carry their shopping home.

The van would be unloaded and housed in its shed; the horses would be taken into the stable, groomed and fed.

In the winter months, when the roads were covered with ice and snow, before making the journey, the horses would be taken to the blacksmith to have frost nails put into their shoes. These would stop, or help to stop, the horses from slipping and sliding about when travelling along slippery roads.'

WALTER 'REG' PARROTT

The Charcoal Maker

'The charcoal burner, whom I found within fifty miles of London, was working a green wood full of dusk and bluebells. A nightingale was singing, the smoke from his hearth drifted up through the shadowy trees, the age-old sound of splashing water and the smell of burning filled the air. He told me he had been a charcoal burner all his life. When he was a grown man and "thought he knew a bit about charcoal", there came an old chap of about eighty, and "taught him something new".

(Made in England, Dorothy Hartley, Methuen
Copyright c. 1939 & Sheil Land Associates)

There is evidence of charcoal making in Britain as far back as 2,500 BC, when there was far more afforestation than today. Used originally as a fuel, it later became an important commodity in the smelting industry, until replaced by coke in the 19th century. Produced in woodlands, and being of light weight relative to its heat output, it was then easier to transport than the wood itself. The charcoal maker might live for several weeks at a time in the woodland, where he would tend several hearths (earth kilns) simultaneously. A hearth might burn for up to a week, and then required raking and cooling. The charcoal maker would erect a make-shift hut in which to live whilst tending (day and night), the hearths. As the wood needed to be dry, charcoal making was a summer-time occupation, and the charcoal maker might have a different occupation during the winter months.

The uses of charcoal and its derivatives over the years are numerous. In addition to its obvious use as a domestic fuel for heating and cooking, it is known to have been used by the Egyptians in embalming, in the production of armour and weaponry, for centuries in smithying and the manufacture of horseshoes, as a preservative (creosote, etc.), as an insulator (the primitive water-cooled 'fridge'), in oast houses in the brewing industry, in the production of armaments, and in batteries. It is still used to produce top-grade steels, and in agriculture, horticulture, water filtration, the pharmaceutical industry, in animal feeds and, as we all know, for barbecues. It is still widely used in developing countries as domestic fuel.

To produce charcoal, wood (or various other materials) must be heated in the absence of air, in order to break down the material chemically. There are many by-products such as tars, oils and naphtha, though these are now mostly produced from oil. What remains is carbon and ash. The cooking process is termed 'exothermic' which means that it generates more heat than it absorbs. When using earth mound kilns, it is necessary to erect screens, which may require re-positioning, to shield the fire from the wind, to slow the burning rate. It is more common now to use a steel kiln, and these measure approximately two metres in diameter and

Demonstrating charcoal-making using a metal kiln, at the Bedfordshire Show, 1994.

two metres in height. These are carefully stacked and the charcoal maker then regulates (by observation and judgement) the rate of carbonisation by adjusting the flow of air into the kiln. On average, six tonnes of wood produces one tonne of charcoal.

Charcoal making creates a useful commodity from waste products of the woodlands, since much wood created by woodland management would have no other use than as fire wood (small wood and if straight enough, wood from upper branches, is known as cordwood) and this is used to produce charcoal.

There was a revivial of charcoal making during the second world war, for use in gas masks. The craft of charcoal making virtually died out prior to this time. Now there is a big demand for charcoal for barbecues. Twenty-eight times as much charcoal is imported into this country as is produced at home mainly because it can be produced far cheaper abroad. (4% home, 96% foreign.)

Charcoal making has an appeal, mainly to those who are independent, and prepared to be at times, solitary characters, according to one such individual, an enterprising young man living in Everton, an electrical engineer, now engaged in charcoal making, whose demonstration at the Bedfordshire Festival aroused much interest.

'Wood is cooked in a metal kiln nowadays: they are a lot more efficient, and it suits today's working methods in this country. Pit kilns are still being used abroad, where earth is covered over the top. You find earth mound kilns, mud brick kilns and many other types. The wood in the kiln is lit, and

Three tonnes of wood about half an hour after lighting.

needs to be got up to temperature quickly. Once up to temperature it can be slowed down and the fire inside runs on the volatile material from the wood; this is a largely self regulating process until it gets to the end of the burning time, when you suffocate it and leave it to cool. The temperature in the metal kilns rises to 500 degrees centigrade, 600 in the middle, and the gases set fire to the tar. The smoke turns blue at this stage and indicates that the cooking process is finished.

Charcoal can be made from any substance that was, or is, living including bones – everything which contains carbon. Any type of tree can be used but it is generally thought the hard woods make a better charcoal, a less soft one with more strength and more carbon, which means it burns for longer. Ash can be made into charcoal quickly, Oak is wet, and greenwood takes time to dry. It is better to allow the sun to do this. Wood needs to be split, as water contained in the wood goes round the rings until it comes to the side which has been split, and this allowed it to escape. This is why firewood is split. When the earth kilns are made the wood was probably

The kilns four hours into the burn

several different lengths but one of the lengths that was used a lot was in a four foot length, which was described as cord wood; a cord was a stack 4 foot by 4 foot by 8 foot long. This term "cord-wood" was an old charcoaling term so it is deduced that quite a bit of wood they used in charcoal making was four foot long. They would have been at some stage making it in coppice woodlands, because in the 1500s there were parts which, because of the devastation with ironworkings and the associated charcoal making, big areas of the country were being depopulated of trees. Laws were brought in to save the woodlands that were left, and these had to be fenced against animals; so the wood was available in these particular areas all the time. If you cut the trees they would sprout again and so the coppice woodlands system was run from that time onwards and probably this length of wood came to be used because it was a convenient length and diameter. The wood supply was probably a harvested commodity rather than a collected commodity. We're using derelict woodlands today which means the timber is way over the size that would have been used in the days when coppice woods were working properly. We're using wood up to sixteen inches in diameter and that has to be split. Coppice wood would just have been put into a kiln.

With the earth type of kiln you have a stack of wood which is usually covered over with something like leaves or straw and earth or turfs packed on top of that and that has to be looked after constantly. Somebody must be there all the time. A friend and I volunteered for this job once, and sat up all night watching the smoke, with the help of our hurricane lamps – which were actually useless because without daylight you cannot see what the smoke is doing. We'd go around looking for holes in the thing but we really couldn't see if what we were looking at, was what we thought we were looking at; or if what we saw was in reality figments of our imagination, in the gloom. You're looking for flames coming out of the holes in the turf, or smoke coming too prolifically in one place instead of the whole thing smouldering smoothly and evenly. It's a skilled operation, learning from others who understand the process. In 1992 this was being done commercially but it is not a sensible way of making charcoal nowadays because the length of time that you spend with it is twenty-four hours a day.

With steel kilns it is a couple of hours when lighting, as you have to wait for the lid to drop, and then you come back next morning to check on it, and then return when you expect it to be done. You spend less time nursing it. It takes about half a day to pack the steel kiln. Each kiln holds about half a ton of charcoal, three cubic metres, and this represents up to five hours loading and five hours preparation of the wood for loading. Preparation is felling, snedding (cutting the trees off the side – some of which will be used in the process), cross cutting (cutting to length), and splitting. That's about a day's work for one man. Then one day's cooking. It requires a day to sit getting cold, and a day to remove, sieve and grade. It is graded for different uses, – for horticulture, for barbecue use, for blacksmithing, but only few blacksmiths use it now.

Charcoal was a big industry until around the turn of the century in this country, but when oil came along it was a lot easier to get the products that people needed from oil rather than from wood. There was quite a lot of charcoal making going on during the war, for use in the manufacture of gunpowder. Speaking of gunpowder manufacture, have you heard the story of the cow pat collectors; apparently, years ago it used to be an offence to touch cow pats before the official collectors had come round, because they used to scrape the white stuff off the top – the saltpetre which was the other ingredient that they needed for gunpowder! The remainder went for infill in timber-framed cottages.

Today we need to market charcoal effectively. Only four percent of charcoal used for barbecues in this country is produced here. We need to educate people about British-produced charcoal and the benefit of using it. The British

Charcoal Group aims to get people talking, because most people in the trade are independent characters who are wary of talking to anyone else. Some co-operation and co-ordination is necessary when you've got so few people doing it. It's a slow matter building credibility and finding outlets. Charcoal gives food a distinctive flavour, which gas doesn't.'

ALISTAIR HOBBS

The Chemist

Before the days of the National Health Service, the local chemist played an important role in advising on the treatment of ailments, and on suitable remedies. Many of the treatments on offer were the chemist's own brand, made up on the premises, and there were also the well-known commercial brands – many of which survive to this day. Tablets were made up after carefully mixing various ingredients, and herbal remedies might also be 'prescribed'. Linaments, inhalants, poultices, antiseptic creams, smelling salts, indigestion remedies, cold and 'flu relief, tummy settlers, tonics and so on. The chemist might also be asked advice on the treatment of animals and pets, and very often the same remedies given to clients would be recommended but in smaller doses. The chemist might also be asked to assist with the fitting of surgical aids and appliances.

There is no doubt that the chemist was held in high esteem by people unable to afford the luxury of a doctor or hospital treatment.

'I left the Grammar School in High Street North, Dunstable in 1925, at the age of sixteen, and began work at Duberley & White in Luton. White was one of the butcher's sons in High Street North. After six months I transferred to the Dunstable Road branch and whilst there, went to evening classes at the old Modern School in Park Square and took part in the qualifying examination. I saved up to go to college – which had to be paid for – that was Westminster College of Pharmacy in Clapham Road. It was just a small college, the

Dunstable Grammar School (now Ashton Middle School), founded in 1887. After its enlargement in 1894 it had provision for 150 boys and 60 boarders. Headmaster: L C R Thring, MA.
Photo: Pub T G Hobbs, Luton & Neighbourhood Illustrated.

Principal of which was P. H. Woodnoth. It was bombed and demolished during the war.
I have worked as a chemist for many years – 1932 until 1987, and the face of pharmacy has changed a great deal during my time. We used to make all manner of treatments and many of our own brands. We also sold perfume and talc and various other things, of course. Almost everything was sold loose then and the ordinary drugs too. You packaged up only what you sold most commonly. Permanganate was a common remedy years ago. Lime water for children, to help form their bones and teeth. Woodwards gripe water was a very popular seller. Beechams Pills and powders "worth a guinea a box". Heringtons, for whom I worked, had their own laxative pills which they advertised on hoardings in the town. Much more then than today, chemists had their own brands.

The first antibiotics were developed after the war: that was the beginning of penicillin. We used to make our own pills and potions. We made ointments and suppositories, and frequently treated children for worms, which they got from the dogs. Boracic acid was used quite a lot in the pharmacy.

In 1912 the Health Service started but only for those earning less that £5, but in 1946 everybody was included. Years ago many doctors had "clubs" and patients paid one penny a week and then if they became ill, there was no charge. Otherwise it was 7/6d per visit. Many more people took advice from the local pharmacist, and were treated by him, and relationships developed over time so that people came to trust his judgement. People used to come from miles around to ask my advice – even from Aylesbury.

The most common ailments which we treated were coughs, colds, chicken pox, whooping cough, bronchitis and pneumonia. Many elderly people suffered with constipation and waterwork trouble. On one occasion I was called out at night – during the war – to a lady whom I thought to be suffering from acute bronchitis or pneumonia. I recommended a treatment and the following day the doctor was called in and he remarked that I had saved the woman's life. Many of the old treatments have died out because they are no longer taught. It used to be common to do three of four years apprenticeship and two years as an assistant before qualifying and during our training doctors came regularly to give us lectures: this was a part of the course.

There used to be quite a lot of veterinary work carried out by local pharmacists. I happened to treat someone's dog at one time, and word got around. We often treated owners and dogs with the same thing – just changed the size of the treatment. We produced our own dog worm and horse worm tablets, horse balls to be pushed down the throat, and hot gruel for cows that had calved. Linseed was a very useful substance. There was no vet at one time, so I often had the task of putting animals to sleep. One Sunday morning I had a cat brought in *which had been run over and I had to put it to sleep before going to church. I've treated many animals, but then there were many fewer vets years ago because people had to pay for their education and training, and money was scarce. The previous vet died aged about ninety and it was several years before another vet came.*

Oxygen cylinders were loaned for use in cases of pneumonia, and returned when they were empty. I've had to take oxygen out to pneumonia cases in a barrow, as you couldn't take them on the bus or tram. They seemed pretty heavy after you'd pushed them two or three miles. I've been out measuring for trusses if the patient couldn't come in. I was taught to measure and fit. Hernias were rarely operated on in those days.

Children knew where to come and be helped. I remember one child came in with a splinter down his thumb. I took off my white jacket so he wouldn't worry, told him to hold my arm and pinch it if I hurt him, and proceeded to remove the splinter. You have to know people and work with them.

It was a most interesting and satisfying profession, and one that provided a valuable service to the community before the National Health Service came into being, and in fact still does.'

ERIC BALDOCK

The Chimney Sweep

Before the days of central heating, the coal fire was not only a universal means of heating homes, but also the means for cooking. A glance at the range of chimney stacks of Victorian properties, and those built up until the 1950s, give some idea of the demand for chimney sweeps. Many chimneys required to be swept twice a year, some once, depending upon the extent of use. There was a time when every home had at least one chimney! It is hard to imagine just how much soot was generated by towns and cities. Much of this soot found its way onto farmland, as fertiliser.

The chimney sweep cycled around with his brushes tied to his cross-bar, and returned home at the end of a long hard day covered in soot, only to wash down and bath in the bungalow bath in front of the kitchen range. He, at least, was one tradesman who could rely on a healthy demand for his services.

'About sixty years ago my wife's uncle lived in Bedford and sold the soot which came from London and which was used on the farms, as fertiliser. He died and I thought I would try the job myself and moved to the country to be near the farms. I lived in Sandy and worked for the Beds Farmers Supply Company in St. Paul's Square, Bedford, and when they finished trading about 1939, I went independent. In those days soot-sowing was a popular way of making extra money. People would ask me which farms I'd sold to, so they could offer their services.

I started chimney sweeping as a part-time venture, and used my tradesman's bike to transport my rods and brushes. I put a notice in a local shop window and it was three weeks until I got my first customer. There was a sweep from Potton and one from Biggleswade doing this area at the time. Business grew and grew, by word of mouth largely, but I did advertise in the local newspapers. In this trade you end up going to different generations of families, and your business grows with the family. If they move, you follow them around. Often customers leave our name for the new owner, and so it goes on.

My son Alan was born in Sandy in 1944 and he joined the business when he left school. There were five of us in the business then, and we had three vans on the road. He worked with his brother-in-law on one van, my other son worked with his cousin in the second vehicle, and I worked on my own with the third. We all worked six days a week, and sometimes seven days. We worked in over one hundred towns and villages then, with five of us working, and even now cover the same amount of area but with just one sweep in our business, which shows the amount of decline in our trade. Our clients included schools, hospitals, churches – boilers or open fires – and bake houses. We had the contract for the Three Counties Hospital in Arlesey, which had two hundred chimneys, and that was done twice a year. Alan always wanted to be a sweep, never thought otherwise, and used to help out during school holidays from about the age of thirteen. It's an interesting job, meeting people, going to different places. No two days are the same. The problem was when my sons and son-in-law went off to do their National Service and I was left on my own. My daughter helped at that time. She used to do the carrying, but she hadn't the strength to push brushes up the chimneys.

When we first started we didn't work with electricity, just rods and brush, and swept up the soot. There were no vacuums. We started using them about fifty-five years ago. A vacuum doesn't sweep the chimney, but just cleans up more efficiently afterwards. There was a firm in Luton which used only a vacuum and they worked in white coats. That firm died a natural death. A vacuum will not sweep the chimney, they will only pick up when the soot is dislodged.

We first put a floor sheet down in front on the fireplace, then bring in the brushes and rods and the cloth which goes over the fireplace. The sheet can be twelve foot wide for inglenooks. We just sweep with the brush and rods, as it has been done for many years. The rods used to be made of cane and the brushes of bass. The rods are now made of polypropylene and the brushes of nylon or one of the plastics. You join the rods as you go, until the brush is pushed through the chimney. That dislodges the soot, which is cleaned up by the vacuum cleaner when you've finished. You push the brush up two or three times, and you can use a scraper. You get a different texture of soot when the client is burning entirely wood. The best quality coal is the dirtiest coal to burn. The lower grade coal makes a smaller amount of soot, but wood soot is the smaller amount of these three. But the problem with wood soot is that is leaves a very hard deposit in the chimney which sometimes even a stiff brush won't dislodge, and a metal scraper has to be used. It sticks on, and becomes like tar, which burns on the inside of the chimney.

Years ago, boys used to climb up the wider chimneys and there were rungs in the chimneys, I believe, or they could wedge themselves across the chimney while they swept by hand. There are no visible means these days for people to climb a chimney, but occasionally it is necessary to clean by hand.

Chimneys go through stages. When Alan started chimney sweeping, thirty-six years ago, on a reasonable size house, a semi, there were three chimneys, the boiler in the kitchen, the lounge, and the dining room chimney, which were used regularly. Then the onset of room heaters came in and domestic boilers which did the radiators, and there was a decline in chimneys. Often there was only a need for one chimney. Chimneys come and go out of fashion. When they were building houses and could sell anything, builders economised on chimneys and fireplaces. When they couldn't sell, the "extras" were chimneys and fireplaces. That was an inducement to buy. There is no class barrier as far as chimneys are concerned. The big houses have a fire which people can sit by in the lounge. Many people by themselves find the fire a great comfort. It gives a good feeling and is company, and elderly people are reluctant to part with their open fire, but when they find they cannot cope with looking after a coal fire, they have to resort to another form of heating. You cannot beat an open fire to sit by with the changing patterns of the flickering flames.

Old places had kitchen ranges when I started. They gradually went out and cooking grates came in, the Triplex, with a fire underneath and an oven on top. Rayburns, the solid fuel oven, which was put in many council houses, and the Rolls-Royce of those was the Aga cooker. The Rayburns did domestic hot water, heated the room and did the cooking.

The modern ones now do the central heating, cooking and domestic hot water.

Modern wood-burning, or multi-fuel stoves are becoming popular now. This industry grew when the Dutch elm disease meant there were many logs to be had and wood-burning stoves came into their own. They are not so popular now due to the fact of the price rise of logs because of the earlier popularity of wood burning stoves. There are various methods of sweeping these. Sometimes they are set in an alcove and where the pipe goes into the chimney there's a cleaning access plate there, or sometimes there is a soot door on the chimney breast itself for access. Sometimes this is set in the outside wall.

Traditionally a fire has been functional, providing heating, airing clothes, heating water, and cooking could be done either on the fire or in the adjoining oven, jacket baked potatoes were done underneath the fire, toasting bread, roasting chestnuts. The dying embers kept the room warm over a long period of time. Ashes could be used as a fertiliser on the garden, clinkers to surface pathways.

Smokeless fuels are not sootless, but you get a different coloured deposit, browns and greys. Conventional coal leaves a black soot. Six chimneys of coal soot would fill one eighty litre bag. We've got sixteen tons of it at my place, at the moment! Only one farmer buys it now, but allotment holders use it. It's sold for 75p for an 80-litre bag, which is not a lot of money, but failing that we would have to pay to dump it. One French polisher used to use it in his stains, but one jar lasted him twenty years!

We have members of parliament on our books. Lady Astor, MP [the first lady to address the House of Commons, on 24.2.1920], she has sons now at Hatley Park village, and we still sweep the chimneys there, regularly. The Pym family in Everton Park, Sandy, we have swept chimneys for three generations, the present owner being the Rt. Hon. Lord Pym. The Queen Mother had a brother who lived at The Gaslings, Southill Park for years, and we swept the chimney there. That was on the Whitbread estate. We did the chimneys for Lady Shuttleworth at the mansion. There is a cross section of people, you can go from the richest to the poorest. I was at The Lodge, Sandy (now the RSPB) at one time and the butler brought me a cup of tea down. The lady of the house, Lady Stuart, came down and saw it and sacked the butler on the spot! We had to use the tradesmen's entrance and try not to be seen nor heard. At Long Stowe Hall near Little Gransden, Lady Bevan makes tea and cakes for us. When I started going there the children's playroom I could have got my house inside. There were Gainsboroughs and other masters hanging on the walls. We've been going there for thirty-six years.

Ordinary people are always welcoming. Another good thing about this trade is that when you go out people know you and are always pleased to see you. The only minus is getting dirty. The only time we mind this is if we have 'flu and know we have to spend three-quarters of an hour cleaning up at the end of the day before we can go to bed, to try to recover ready for the next day's work. Whatever village or town you go to, people recognise you and speak, even if you are not working.

If a coal fire is used for heating, and during the day, and during the cold weather, then it should be swept twice a year. For evening and weekend use, once a year. We just judge them on their merits.

Fortunately chimney fires are rare. It doesn't just depend upon the quantity of soot in the chimney, a bit of soot can be set on fire as easily as a lot of soot. Soot can easily be set on fire. A lot of soot can burn for a couple of hours and you can't touch your hand on the wall of the chimneys throughout the house. People in rented houses used to set chimneys on fire to reduce the soot in the chimney, but it causes damage to the chimney. If it happens now, it is usually by accident. If the property is thatched the sparks will rain down on the roof and it is best to get the fire brigade as soon as you can. If there is not much soot, you can dampen it out and stuff a wet sack into the chimney, which will help to keep it under control until it goes out or until you get help. It stops the red-hot soot falling out and holds it at bay until help arrives.

With inglenooks, a three-foot diameter brush is used and very stout rods. It starts off very wide at the base of the chimney but by the time you get up to about ten feet height it is a respectable size, but for the lower part you get into the bottom and use a hand-brush to brush out what the rods have missed. You start with the rods and resort to the handbrush for anything you have missed. The days of putting boys up the chimney have gone and it is illegal, but we have to go into some chimneys ourselves. In this job you don't need to worry about dieting, as the continuous exercise seems to burn off the calories.

You need to bath and wash your hair every day. Years ago showers were not popularly used, and when I started we had a bath every day in a bungalow bath in front of the fire. We sweeps were cleaner than most! When you are covered in soot you need something in the water like a little Fairy Liquid or something to counteract the grease. We have used soda in the

The author's granddaughter, Jordan, still enjoying the delights of the bungalow bath.

water in times gone by. We wear boiler suits but the soot goes through it. Soot gets everywhere. We leave our top clothes in the outhouse when we get home, and there's a handbasin there for a preliminary wash and change before coming into the house.

Years ago, four of us swept twenty chimneys on a Sunday at Shire Hall in Bedford. They preferred Sunday because no-one was working, and the caretaker would be there to let us in.

We had a contract with RAF Henlow. The married quarters were swept four times a year. The wooden billets that had felted and tarred roofs – which was a fire risk – contained three tortoise stoves, which were swept from the top, even when the fires were alight. They were cleaned fortnightly, the soot just dropping onto the fire. These stoves only had a small smoke pipe so burning coal meant they soon got sooted-up.

At the Three Counties Hospital the wards were self-contained, with the bedded area, dining and lounge, and bathroom. It was not unusual to have twelve chimneys on a ward. That was their form of heating. With the night staff there on cold nights and burning fuel overnight, they had big fires and that must have meant big bills.

Our prices vary according to the type of chimney. Ordinary lounge fires are £8. When I started it was 4d or 6d. The most difficult would now be £15. It is not unrare to find jackdaws' nests in inglenooks. There is one at Gransden which produces three dustbins full of jackdaws' nests each year. Starlings are also found in chimneys. A nest blocks a chimney completely so no smoke goes up.

Because of the fall in demand, there is only one person running the business now, my son Alan, but it is still a full-time occupation. He sometimes attends weddings for friends and for customers whose daughters are getting married. It's a long-standing tradition to greet the bride as she comes out of the church and give her a kiss as good luck, which is why you often see a bride given a good luck charm of a chimney sweep. People ring up and ask him to come to the

'Good luck will rub off when I shakes hands with you!' Alan at the wedding of Adrian Green and Tracey Lawson.

wedding. Bridegrooms ring up and arrange it occasionally, or the bride's sisters. He often attends weddings for the sisters when their turn comes. He wears a white glove so when he shakes hands they don't get dirty, but the bride gets her kiss. We make a cover charge for doing weddings, as you need to see the church first to see where you can hide, and you can be at the church for an hour or two, waiting for the right opportunity. It is time-consuming, but a nice occasion. Alan has been invited to the reception too, but that means coming home to change first. He has only done this once, for a friend's son. His own two children are getting married this year, but he will only be there in one role, and not as the lucky sweep.'

RICHARD 'DICK' BARROWS

The Clock and Watch Repairer

In modern times watches can cost very little, having built-in obsolescence. Use and throw away. Those of us maintaining more expensive watches, or watches with sentimental value, will find that repairs are costly. Before the age of digital clocks and electronic movements, watches were crafted mechanical time-pieces. In the early years of the century a wristwatch was a source of pride, and something not everyone could afford. Watches were frequently given as gifts, and as a token of gratitude for long service a retiring employee would occasionally be given a gold watch. The watch required periodic cleaning, servicing and adjustment, and the clock and watch repairer was to be found in most communities.

In addition to repairing watches (and occasionally crafting

replacement parts), the repairer would also offer a home-visiting service in order to service more ornate clocks which were better not removed, unless repair on site was not possible. Grandfather and other cased clocks frequently required servicing and adjustment.

A typical parlour shop, still trading today.

'I was apprenticed in London with P. Julius & Son Ltd, from January 1943. Julius Purchen was the owner; he was a Russian Jew from Kiev, who came to this country at the turn

of the century as a young man. He originally had a kiosk in Praed Street, near Paddington Station, and later traded from 11 & 11a Praed Street.

During the war-time years everything was in short supply. You could not buy new clocks and had to have a permit to buy alarm clocks. There was obviously a big demand for repairs. I started with Julius repairing clocks, and progressed into watches and other mechanisms. During those days you could get certain parts, but there were many you couldn't get and which had to be made by hand to suit the requirements. This is how I learnt my craft, working with a treadle lathe, turns, etc. Many of the methods I was taught originated from the earlier days, because my employer did his apprenticeship at the end of the last century. He had trays of jewellery, a huge selection of high class watches and clocks. He had a good reputation and people came to him from all walks of life, Harley Street specialists and many other notable people, including Alexander Flemming, who was based at St. Mary's–Paddington Hospital.

Julius's son Abbie Purchen had a shop opposite. Alex, another son who worked with this father, suffered badly with asthma. He died before his father, and I can still remember his father crying behind the counter. He was heart-broken. It was such an old shop, and rats used to come up from the cellar and sit above the curtain rail which draped behind the

71

bench area. Customers could watch the work in progress, behind the bench. It was during this time, that I met my future and present wife, Rosina. She was very experienced in the spare parts trade, obtaining required components from Clerkenwell, taking items to gold and silver merchants, etc. She worked for Julius for ten years and has always been of great assistance to me.

I went into the Merchant Navy for a while and when I left, started working privately, doing watch repairs at home. I did a lot of work for Walker's the Jewellers. They used to batch up their work and send it out for repair. I have had other work, but continued privately at home.

My wife had a friend who worked for Purdy's in South Kensington, and she brought home batches of watches for me to repair. Purdy had been a First World War fighter pilot. He offered me a job and I worked for him for two years doing straightforward watch repairs, much of it on antiques, watches and clocks. Whilst I was working for Purdy's, I used to go out to customers in South Kensington to look at clocks. In those

Popular in the 1940s and '50s, this Nell Gwyn reproduction clock was possibly made originally in the 1600s.

Pocket watch assortment, including silver case key-winds.

Gravity Clock. The actual weight of the clock is used to drive it. When the clock slides to its lowest point, it is raised up in order to rewind it. They were only manufactured for a short time, and were made in solid brass.

73

early days, just after the war, I had a motorbike combination, which I used for travelling around to customers. Often I could make adjustments on the spot, or else the clocks would be brought back to the shop for full repair. Many of these were wealthy clients. A lot of them had mechanical clocks with singing birds and other decorative objects. One had a ship which appeared to be in a stormy sea, and the ship would pitch and roll when the clock chimed. We used chicken skin to get the sea effect, when we repaired and restored it. There were all types of musical boxes and such a variety of clocks, a variety of makes.

Mrs Moira Scott was a good customer. She was a very old lady, who was most appreciative, and used to give me various things for my children when I called to do her repairs. Many of our customers had several clocks, and there were lots of Grandfather clocks. They needed repairing and servicing. There were beautiful Dutch clocks with paintings on, regulators and bracket clocks. Also large numbers of carriage clocks. Besides clocks, there were many antique and old watches such as Verge, English Lever, Repeaters, etc. I remember going out to one elderly lady who was an alcoholic and who insisted there was something at the bottom of her Grandfather clock. It was full of cobwebs at the bottom, but I groped around and found a big empty gin bottle. She had hidden bottles everywhere. Haigh, the mass murderer whose victims were wealthy people, usually elderly, had been staying at the Onslow Hotel in Pelham Street before his arrest, and some of our customers came from the hotel. When he was caught, one of the ladies remarked to us, what a nice man he was. She didn't appear to be aware that she herself was a prospective victim! He used acid vats to dispose of his victims, and had a yard in one of the Mews. This was just up the road from where I worked.

From about 1950, I worked for Smiths at Cricklewood, in their Watch and Clock Service Department. I remained there for ten years, working on clocks, watches, chiming clocks, pigeon racing clocks, etc. I also travelled around to special customers as part of the service. One customer for repairs was Lord Trenchard. His home was part of the Royal Establishment. He was in charge of air-affairs during the war. A Smith pigeon racing clock came out about that time. It was called a Sky-master and I received some special training at the factory of manufacture. The rac-ing pigeon wears a

A jewelled watch movement.

rubber ring which is numbered and fitted around its leg, prior to being released at the race start point. When the pigeon arrives at his/her home destination the owner removes the ring and places it into a thimble which then wound into the clock. The clock registers the time of insertion to the second, by making inked stamp marks on a roll of paper, which cannot be removed except by official checkers. A Skymaster would take ten thimbles, i.e. ten pigeon rubber rings. Pigeon racing was a popular sport and hobby. I have done repairs on these and other makes since being in Luton, where there was a Pigeon Racing Club, as there were in many parts of the country. The Skymaster was banned for a period at one time because it allowed cheating. The timing in the clock could be altered by shaking the clock and therefore people could cheat when recording flight times, and pigeon racing was a form of gambling with high rewards. Eventually a device called a dolometer was fitted internally to the clock, which recorded shaking, and therefore disqualification from a race. Something like 20,000 of those clocks were produced. We also repaired stop watches, specially designed for different sports such as Yacht Racing, etc.

I moved to Dunstable from London in 1958 whilst I was working for Smiths. At that time we were using steam trains. I was often stuck in fog in London and after a long train journey, didn't get home until late at night. I eventually started working for Kents Instruments in Biscot Road, Luton, as an Instrument Maker. They had a Swiss jig borer on which I did specialised precision work, and a lot of work for the Admiralty. I also worked in their Research and Development Department, creating model patterns for designers. At that stage I was employed as a Model Shop Technician. In later years I worked for Leitz in Park Street, Luton as a Camera Technician, repairing cameras including the very expensive "M" Series – Leica camera, whose original prototype was designed in 1913. I remained with Leitz until my retirement.

Most watches and clocks nowadays are electronic, few having moving parts any more. Years ago we used to do servicing and repairs, gilding, engraving, enamelling and rhodium plating. We worked with diamonds and jewels. Clerkenwell Road and Hatton Garden in London was an area renowned for clock and watch dealing.'

NORMAN DRURY

1948 advertisement for J L and J W Purdy, 9 Pelham Street, Kensington.

'I was born in Dover, over my father's jeweller's shop and as I grew up, I spent many hours in father's workshop. When the war began, our shop was closed and the family moved to Dunstable. I transferred from Dover County School to Dunstable Grammar, and on leaving school, went to work for my father, doing general repair work.

In the early part of the war stock was reasonable, but as the war progressed it became al-

Walker's in Middle Row, Dunstable, shortly after the war.

most unobtainable, and thus many items of clocks, watches and jewellery which had been "retired" years before, were brought back into service. The usual good-quality clocks, Vienna Wall, French Strikes and timepieces, chime, strikes and eight-days, were still repaired, but worn and damaged ones, normally bought for replacement parts, were not available. Even alarm clocks were available only to essential workers, so many of these were done.

With the shortage of stock also came the shortage of available spares, some of which were imported, but many made in this country by skilled personnel were now unobtainable, since most of them had now been drafted to the *forces or the factories. So tools of the trade which had laid idle for many years were returned to service. I remember particularly an old pair of watchmaker's turns (an early type of hand-operated lathe), being returned, having been idle for some twenty years.*

Many parts which would normally have been replaced now had to be repaired or made by hand. This may sound rather primitive, but many private and company shops had only very limited facilities on site, as most work, before and since the war, was sent either to central workshops or to outworkers. Thus many clocks and watches were saved from the scrap heap. I remember nine carat "Utility" broad or narrow, as the only available wedding rings, which were later platinum-lined, to make them more "valuable". I also remember being reprimanded for over-selling our very limited stocks!

On returning from the Forces I returned to the retail and management side of the trade, and finally retired three years ago, having served forty-nine years in the trade.'

RON WITHERALL (born 16.4.1927)

Two of the clocks from Ron's personal collection.

The Coal Merchant

Every home required coal for fires and ranges, and even after central heating became popular, solid fuel was a common form of heating. Wood and coal-burning stoves, Agas for heating and cooking, all demanded regular deliveries of coal.

Schools, hospitals and other institutions continued to use solid fuel heating even after the second world war. Only with increased imports of oil, and the use of natural gas, has demand for coal diminished.

Coal brought to Bedford by rail, was collected, bagged, and delivered to towns and villages by horse and cart not so many years ago, and then by lorry. The coalman was a busy man providing an essential service to the community.

Different grades of coal, different sizes, lumps to facilitate storage, all had to be carried to the coalhouse, yard, or coalbunker. Summer deliveries at reduced prices, winter deliveries in rain, winds, and snow, the coalman was a hardy tradesman, used to carrying heavy loads and working in all conditions and able to brave the elements.

'Our business was originally started by my grandfather, Thomas David Boyles, who was born in 1864. He started work as 'orse-keeper for Randalls Brickyard in Stewartby, before 1900, although it weren't known as Stewartby then.

Coalcart in Littledale, Kempston, early 1920s.

'E wanted to be independent and to be 'is own boss, and gave up his job. 'E used to say that when 'e gave in 'is notice and collected his cards, they didn't even say "thank you". 'E then started as a coalman, at the age of thirty-six, and the business was called T. D. Boyles. This was about 1900.

Me grandfather built up his rounds and got work by word of mouth. There was another coalman in Wootton, later, a Mr Robinson, but not any competition really. Most places 'e 'ad, 'ad got a field and 'e used to rent some ground. As far as I know 'e kept a cow and a pig or two, for 'is own consumption. 'E used to live in 'oo Lane, Wootton Green, Bott End near Potters Cross, then from my time 'e lived at Folly Farm, Keeley, opposite the Rose an' Crown. As well as coal deliveries 'e did other work on 'is farm or smallholding, there were two grass fields, still is now. 'E collected coal from Bedford, from John E. Page, Coal Merchant, and 'ad to go to Bedford Railway Station to load. It's now the car park to County 'all. 'E always 'ad fairly regular customers and also used to do the council schools, and me father did too, but stopped doing them because we weren't willing to reduce our prices. They only paid ya once or twice a year and this was not satisfactory. If ya put the coal in just after payday ya 'ad to wait nearly six months for ya money.

Me grandfather used to wear thick shirts for work, without collars. 'E 'ad no other shirts. For best 'e wore a shirt-front "bib" which was white, and 'ad a collar attached, and this 'e wore over his working shirt. 'E 'ad thick suits made for work, and long-sleeved waistcoats so when delivering, 'e took off his jacket and worked in 'is long-sleeved waistcoat, in cold weather. It was a thick twill material, and very warm. 'E usually wore a sack tied around his waist whilst at coalcart.

Collecting the coal was an arduous task. Pages loaded, with our assistance, into our own bags. On a four wheel trolley, a load was a ton to twenty-five hundredweight. You needed a good 'orse to go to Wootton, and we delivered mainly in the Wootton and Kempston area. You could collect one load and deliver in Kempston, return to re-load and then stop for lunch. There were brick offices in the coal yard where you 'ad your lunch. You carried a nosebag on your trolley, for the 'orse. The second load was delivered in the afternoon in the Wootton area. Then it'd be 4 o'clock and you'd go back to bed down the 'orse and 'ave a cup of tea and then milk the cows.

Grandfather was strict with the animals. There was straw in the stable for each 'orse and you 'ad to dry the 'orse with a whisk of straw and rub it down before you 'ad your tea, on a pouring wet day. "Dumb animals can't look after themselves" 'e would say. You gave the 'orse a little pan with two double 'andfuls of rolled oats and a little chaff at one feed and went back twenty minutes later, looked in the manger an' if there was any long bits of chaff left you swept them to one side and gave it a repeat feed. You done that per'aps three or four times. It 'ad to eat up and clear it before getting more, so it couldn't bolt food and get griped. Once it was digested they could 'ave more. In winter they was kept in the stables and at 7 o'clock they 'ad a bucket with so much bran in, linseed cake, 'ot water, which was allowed to cool, and that was the last meal of the night, "bran mash". Grandfather kept some of the 'orses which 'e 'ad for many years, and cared for them in retirement. Others would be part-exchanged, but 'e kept the long-surviving ones and cared for them. They 'ad three at any one time. Two carts (one was me uncle Will's), and two trolleys, before we went over to lorries. The cart doubled up as an 'arvesting vehicle: three 'orses, cart and trolleys. This was for 'arvesting 'is own corn, as 'e 'ad nine acres at North Field near Potters Cross. 'E rented this land from the parish council, who rented it from Vauxhall's.

Country people stored coal in the barns, or tipped it outside. Some was purchased in big pieces, lumps, for ease of storage, or tipped out from the bags into barns or coal bunkers. Sometimes people would leave out a brush and bucket of water so that we could sweep up the coaldust and swill down the yard before leaving. Most deliveries were during the

Corn cutting with a binder. Maurice's cousin Edgar is on the front horse, and his father is driving the horses.

Maurice's father at coalcart, 1947, delivering to the School House at Wootton School, and carrying lumps.

summer. One to four tons per year could be consumed by any one 'ouse'old. This was the main form of 'eating years ago.

Me father was Thomas Charles Boyles, known as "Charlie". When 'is brother William came out of the army in 1918 there wasn't much work for all of 'em, so me father went on to a farm at Keeley Corner. 'Is brother then started on his own as a coal merchant with a lorry, and me father returned to the business to work with 'is father in the 1920s. Father married in 1927 and bought a

Maurice's father, who used to do a lot of shooting (rabbits, hares, and game), and sold to order.

thatched cottage in 1930, called Deep Thatches, 95 Keeley Lane, Wootton, where 'e lived until 'e died in 1990. 'E used to say how his father used to knock on the bedroom door at 4.00 in the morning and if he wasn't down by ten past, 'e would call up "are ya layin' in bed all day then". They 'ad to deliver milk to Kempston to sell in bulk, in churns, before starting with the coal rounds. Father delivered with an 'orse and cart, and their carts were maintained by Redman the wheelwright at Keeley Corner and Bedford Road. In 1948 me uncle Will was ill and couldn't carry coal again, and me father took over 'is business as well, and they used a lorry as well as the carts, as the workload 'ad doubled. It was a Commer van made for

Maurice's father's home in Keeley Lane, Wootton.

Commer van, bought 1948. It was purchased by an enthusiast, and restored.

the airforce, who never took delivery of it. It 'ad a split windscreen, unlike the civilian version, and twin fan belts, with a twenty-four gallon tank, as opposed to the normal twelve gallon, and 'ad a dipstick as a fuel gauge. It were made at the end of the second world war, and we bought it in 1948.

It was about 1948 when me father finished working in the business, and concentrated on the smallholding and on pig breeding. 'E bred and sold at about twelve weeks old. Some 'e sold to Mr 'yde of 'oughton Conquest, and they went abroad to Bermuda to appear in a film. They all 'ad to be the same colour, grey and white, and 'e bred 'em from a pure-bred black sow and white boar. They done a bit in the Beds Times, and the reporter said that me father spoke with "a rich Bedfordshire accent not encountered so often these days". Me

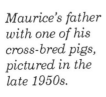

Maurice's father with one of his cross-bred pigs, pictured in the late 1950s.

father raised store cattle, kept poultry, produced eggs, and grew cereals, corn, oats and barley. 'E retired from the coal business in 1968, and I then ran the business myself. 'E didn't drive ya see, but I did, so 'e concentrated on the pigs.

From 1948 I was doing about five to eight tons a day by using the lorries. August was a slack period because we were 'arvesting. There was a reduction of price from May until about October or November. May, June and July were busy months and the rest of the customers bought in the winter. Some customers only 'ad a delivery in the summer and that lasted them through the year. In the order of five- to six-hundred customers we 'ad at any one time. Whilst the controls were in force coal was rationed to thirty-four 'undredweight per year. They could have ten deliveries of three bags and one of four 'undredweight, making thirty-four 'undredweight in twelve months, and it gave us a month free to do the 'arvesting work, cutting the corn and stacking it.

In the later 1980s business began to dwindle. They didn't put gas on in many villages until about the middle 1980s. In the last few years it reduced, until about 1990 it was 'ardly a living. This was one reason I finished, as there was little profit. Then me father died in 1990, me son having married in 1989 and then I was on me own. Then two of me cousins died and I decided it was time to relax! Your working day was about 8.00 in the morning, finishing about 4.00 to 4.30. Me lunch break was usually brief, because it weren't very pleasant sitting in a cold vehicle eating ya sandwiches.

Years ago it was mostly ordinary 'ousehold coal, about four grades, but then in the 1950s closed fires came in, so there was coal and coke and manufactured fuels. Towards the end, it was mostly manufactured fuels which were smokeless. Manufactured coal was more expensive. Many people changed to gas for convenience.

Coal was about three shillings for a one 'undredweight bag when I started at fifteen, because I can remember a customer giving me a ten shilling note for three bags and father always gave me the change to 'and over. Grandfather delivered at eightpence a bag or tenpence for the best graded stuff when 'e started.

There were miners strikes at times and the general strike, and there was no coal, but people felled trees in Wootton and father changed over to wood deliveries at this time.

Mrs Newbury at Wood End always 'ad the kettle on as you pulled up. It was a regular thing to 'ave a cup of tea and we got to know our customers well. We'd put the nosebag on the 'orse and take a break. The old people, especially, were welcoming and also where you delivered a ton or two in the summer they would usually ask you in for a drink. The old chap would come running out with bucket and spade as we left, to scoop up the 'orse's droppings for the garden.

When they went metric the bags were slightly lighter. I still found it as easy to carry at the end of my working life as I did at the beginning, but couldn't do it now, after a break. I retired in October 1991.'

MAURICE BOYLES

The Cobbler

For years, traditional footwear was leather. From childhood people wore leather boots and shoes. Old leather softens and conforms to the shape of the foot, and thus shoes and boots were handed down to younger children in a family, and would last for years. The hobnail slowed down the rate of wear, saving on repair costs. Nothing was thrown away until repair was no longer a viable proposition.

The Victorian and Edwardian family walked to school, work, the shops, etc. and walked for pleasure. Streets and footpaths were not in the condition they now are. Potholes, puddles, cobblestones, unmade country roads! Strong, water-proof leather footwear was essential, and this was an investment. Repairs could often be carried out by father, using a last, or shoes would be sent to the cobbler. The cobbler trade flourished and cobblers were to be found in every locality. Secondhand leather boots could be purchased from the cobbler, at the secondhand shop or from the pawn shop. Children from poor families often possessed no more than one pair of shoes and one hears of absence from school because shoes were in for repair.

Odells, Cobblers, in St. Cuthbert's Street, Bedford, originally comprised three cottage dwellings, and at the turn of the century, these were a sweet shop, the cobblers, being the central cottage, and on the other end, a dwelling house. In 1916 the shoe repairer was drafted into the Forces and the shop was put up for sale. At the same time Alfred Odell, the founder of the present business, had been made redundant from the shoe factories in Kettering. He moved to Bedford and bought the business.

Alfred Odell had two sons, Bertram Edward and Lesley Martyn, both of whom came into the family business. It is believed they lived in the end cottage at one time. Alfred died in the early 1930s and the sons took over. While Alfred was in charge the sweet shop became vacant and he bought it, and the end prop-

Chesher & Son, Boot Makers, Howard's Avenue, Queens Park, 1905. The cobbler is believed to be Bert Chesher.
Photo: courtesy Mr D Markham.

Alfred Odell (left), at the shop in 1920.

erty. When he died he owned all three properties. Bertram died in the early 1960s, Lesley died in the early 1970s. Lesley's son, Kenneth Alfred, took over the business in the 1970s and carried on until he died very suddenly in 1989 aged about sixty-two. He had worked in the business since leaving school and was looking forward to his retirement. He was a bachelor. Lesley's son and daughter, David and Sandra, were not interested in continuing the business and it was sold. Mr Hammond, a local businessman, bought this business in order to preserve it. He had the building listed and improved the fabric of the building whilst retaining the character. Odells has now diversified and stock various items associated with the shoe trade, and is an agent for dry cleaning.

Derek Bishop joined Odells' family business after leaving school in 1953. He has succeeded the Odell family, to become head repairman of the present business.

Mr Bishop, the cobbler, still providing a personal service, using traditional methods complemented by new techniques.

'Several factors have brought about the demise of the cobbler. Built-in obsolescence is one factor. Ever since the "trainers" appeared in the 1970s, shoes have been designed to be worn and thrown away. Trainers alone halved the repair trade. When the Odells owned the business there were about a hundred pairs a day coming into the shop: now this is around twenty-five pairs. The same with "joggers" and other imported shoes. The thick soles and heels ensure that the shoes will not require repair and, as the uppers wear out before the soles, the shoes are thrown away and replaced. Stilettoes boosted trade in their day, because they wore out in weeks and needed to be repaired. Doc Martins-type shoes have done the trade no good at all either. Years ago everybody wore leather shoes and boots, including school children. With poor people, fathers used to do the repairs but if they could afford it they sent their shoes to the local cobblers to be done. Bedford had about ninety shoe repairers in the 1940s. Every street had its shoe repairers, most one-man businesses. There were about three in Castle Road, several in the side streets and a number in the town centre. Boggas's, a big shoe repair business in Bedford, had shops in several villages around Bedford: the main one was in Midland Road. They used to repair army boots during the war as well as civilian work. There were shops of theirs in Ampthill and other places. Welsh was another big business in Bedford, and they had several shops. Most of these shops were started off because of the war, because they got army contract work or RAF work, especially as there were camps in Kempston and Cardington. Demand for repairs was great. These businesses got established and carried on after the war but most have packed up now.

We now look around the villages for agents. You can't rely on people coming in the shop door. In 1953 when I started, there were about a dozen people here, and now there are three.

When I first came we used to do Major Simon Whitbread's shoes [High Sheriff], the Gales, who were big ironmongers [now Gibbs and Dandy], doctors' shoes, professional people. Our client is the sort of person who buys good leather shoes and wouldn't want them to go to a heel bar with staple fixing by a young lad who is untrained. There is no personal touch. A lot of people who come here we know by name and they have been coming for years. One lady, Miss Perks, of The Grove, she has been coming here for the best part of seventy years. She can remember when this was a sweet shop.

I came in 1953 straight from school – Goldington Road Secondary Modern. I was fifteen. I didn't have a bound apprenticeship: mine was an ordinary apprenticeship of about five years. With a bound apprenticeship you signed a contract *and were obliged to stay for five years. That's why you didn't go into National Service until the age of twenty-one, otherwise you went into the army at eighteen, which I did, for two years. When I started, you worked forty-four hours for forty-four shillings, were obliged to take a medical under the Factories Act. Dr Halliday whose surgery was in Mill Street, was appointed as being a factories doctor. My employer paid for the examination. I was taught the trade for an unspecified period of time, and this training was not certificated.*

I still use the same screwdriver and hammer which I started with. The employer bought a set of basic tools for a new apprentice – pinchers, screwdriver and odds and ends. This was the starting kit. Then you watched the cobbler repair shoes: he showed you the stages, what to do and you copied and gradually worked through all the stages of shoe repairing.

Our main supplier for the trade was Baileys of Kettering,

Working on the blake machine, which is one hundred years old. Originally operated by treadle, it has now been converted to electric. There is one on display in the Shoe Museum at Northampton.

who supplied the bulk of the material. The representative came once every five weeks to take the order. The leather may have been tanned and produced in the area, Northampton, Rushden: it came in large "bends" which were cut up here on the premises with a press, in the early days, all the soles and the heels. As the years went by it became cheaper to buy them already cut. Now it comes from Marshall Coppin Ltd., Wholesalers, from Sutton. Probably much is imported from Italy and other places.

We still use glue and nails, nothing is stapled on. We remove the part which is worn, build up if necessary so as to be level, and then the top piece is stuck on, shaped then nailed, as it has always been done. It is finished off on the machine, which is a very old-fashioned one. The heel would be smoothed and shaped to fit, then stained, then polished. With leather soles the old ones are taken off and a new one stuck on. In the case of welted shoes the new sole would be trimmed, channelled, stitched onto the welt and the channel closed, levelled down and finished, the sole shaped, the edges stained or inked. That is the old-fashioned, proper way of doing it, in my opinion. This is what people like. If you have a hundred pound pair of shoes you would like to think they were being done properly, especially people who work in offices and have good quality shoes and want to keep them. We repair shoes which have probably been soled half a dozen times. They might have had a pair of shoes twenty years, and they are still coming back to be repaired.

People walk less now that they did forty or fifty years ago. Many families didn't have a car and people walked greater distances. Today people drive to the shop and park out front. Even children go to school on buses. More people are walking for leisure now, and many do long-distance walking. It's becoming more popular. We get quite a few walking, rambling and climbing boots in for repair. A good pair of boots for this purpose costs a hundred pounds. In the last five years or so manufacturers have produced lightweight walking boots gortex lined. These are made by W Gore of Scotland. Gortex is a thin material which lets out the perspiration but doesn't let in the rain. It allows the feet to breathe.

The demise of the trade began in the early 1960s with moulded rubber boots and Tuf boots and shoes. These were revolutionary, and guaranteed for six months free of repair. Industrial boots and army boots. Up until then the army boots were leather, with studs. Parade boots are still leather but others are moulded rubber.

Times haven't changed greatly. I've done repairs on hobnail boots, soled and heeled them and put hobnails in. Hobs or triple hobbs. These slowed down the length of time between repairs. The cobblers' lasts are still used even though these can be seen in museums. We still use the revolving punch for making holes in uppers, eyelets, etc., and the patching machine for stitching uppers which have come undone. The basic tools of the trade are still the same.'

DEREK BISHOP

Odell's shop in St. Cuthbert's Street is about three hundred years old, and when it was built and for years afterwards this was a residential area. Now it is mainly com-

Alfred Odell.

mercial. On the morning when the new owner took over, a runaway lorry hit the end of the building, which caused a lot of damage. The whole of the gable end had to be repaired and the sides were shored up and foundations created where none existed previously, this being a rendered timber-framed building with wattle and daub and horsehair infill. the building is now structurally sound and various renovation work has been sympathetically carried out so as to maintain the character of the premises and of this very traditional business which the new owner intends to continue virtually unchanged.

In the early nineties when the south end was rebuilt a time capsule was put in the cavity with records of Odell's and the staff, together with newspapers, etc.

The Coppice Worker

Coppice is the term used to describe a wood of low trees. It consists of quick-growing wood which is cut at various stages of its growth, in order to be used to make various artifacts. The woods most commonly grown for coppicing were ash, hazel, oak and chestnut. The coppice worker was involved in woodland management and, working in the woodland, he produced both tools and artifacts from coppice wood, which were then collected and transported from site.

Hazel can be used for making wattle hurdles for sheep or horses, for thatching spars, and rods: ash for sheep hurdles, horse jumps and gate hurdles, for gates, hay rakes, tent pegs and rods. Oak is used in cleft oak fencing, for stakes and rustic work.

'Coppice originated thousands of years ago. Some early hurdles used for firm roadways over the fens date from five thousand years ago. The same technique is used today. By the Bronze Age, all the wood-working tools had been developed. Some Bedfordshire woods have been used for coppice for three thousand years, and are still in use. One wood in the Lake

District had over two hundred different products, from houses to block and tackle, even ropes. There were many different craftsmen in Bedfordshire in medieval times, many crafts now being lost.

The type of wood in the coppice determines the types of crafts carried out. In Bedfordshire most old woods were oak, ash, hazel, or elm hazel. The elm and oak were left as timber trees until one hundred and sixty years old, then sold by the owner. Coppice workers took the "lops and tops" or bits the timber merchant did not want. Oak from branches made oak spale baskets, dowel pegs. Look at an old house and see how the curved branches have been used as braces, brackets, etc. Oak was the rich man's coffin, elm the poor man's coffin. Elm was the commonest tree in Bedfordshire until Dutch Elm Disease. Cart wheel hubs, boats, floors and platters, bowls, tankards, bridges. The Alder woods near Flitwick were used for clog soles, made into hurdles for holding river banks, piles or boats. Ash made tools such as spades when iron was so expensive only the edge could be made of iron. Tool handles, wheel spokes, furniture and many more.

Maple remains a mystery, but coppice of maple is common in parts of the County. Another mystery are coppices of hornbeam all round London. Both may have been grown for hop poles, though maple is used for fine work and furnishings. There are some beech in parts of the county for furniture, though beech or maple pulleys set in elm blocks were used by the hundred in sailing ships. Sweet chestnut does not grow well in the county, but horse chestnut has been used in ceiling beams, especially in cowsheds and dairies. Horse chestnut is supposed to repel flies.

Willow of all types was grown in osier beds or as Pollards on river and stream banks. Biggleswade had five basket making firms, one employing twelve men. Fruit and vegetables were sold in baskets woven locally, with basket-work chairs popular for relaxation. Some cricket bat willow was grown along the Ouse. Willow was made into bobbins, or into chip baskets for fruit. Hazel was used for thousands of hurdles before the land enclosure of the nineteenth century to fold sheep on the unfenced fields. Ash hurdles were used for cattle, usually young stock. Thatching required thousands of hazel spars to hold the thatch. Poles, bean sticks, and pea sticks, were the last real use for some woods, but thatching and hurdle making is still in existence. Some basket work is done, and more osier beds could be commercially viable today.

So many things were made of wood, and all cooking and heating relied on wood fires until the canals and trains brought cheap coal. So important was wood in Medieval times that laws protecting trees were passed. Anyone felling or damaging trees could have a hand cut off. Coppice comes from the Domesday Book, and meant a wood that was cut (Coupe = cut) as against forét grown for timber, or chassuer for hunting. Look at a map and the chases, forests and coppices can be seen today.

Stone age man armed with flints used small trees for ease of cutting. Wattle and daub lasted thousands of years, though each hut had to be rebuilt every fifteen years. After the bronze age, larger trees were used as frame, and filled in with wattle and daub. Bedfordshire has some good stone in the northwest, but the rest only has soft chalk. Wooden-frame houses lasted after the river navigation brought cheap sawn deal for houses, with lath and plaster or cement to waterproof the outside. The black and white of old houses was black tar on the frame, and lime cement on the wattle and daub.

Stone age man had invented most tools used today, and bronze, later iron tools of the same shapes were made. Steel is comparatively recent. Archaeologists puzzled over the odd shapes of bronze age tools until a group saw me at work at the East of England Show with those same tool shapes. I could show them how to use them. A good coppice worker still works in the wood with equipment made on the spot, and few basic tools such as bill hook, axe and adze, wedges and beetle for

Tools of the coppice trade, on display at the Bedfordshire Show, 1994.

cleaving logs, and until the 1960s, pole lathes turning out chair parts or tool handles. Clog makers and crate makers still came round after the war. Now crafts such as cooperage are being lost as craftsmen grow old and die off.

Today we see the last few crafts and craftsmen. Hazel spars for thatching are still in demand, and the odd gate or wattle hurdle is made for ornament. Ancient coppice woods are "conserved" and so not now available to the coppice workers, much to the detriment of both. It was Henry the Eighth that ruled a coppice worker cut standard trees, those where he could span round with his fingers: about five inches diameter these days. All trees belonged to the king as owner of all lands. Now all trees belong to the landowner under the same law. Craftsmen were freemen who paid for coppice by work in the harvest and sowing times, selling their hurdles in return for corn or meat. There are records of the same family using the same wood for five hundred years, for thatching spars. Generations of a family would follow the craft, and coppice was well looked after. Cheap transport and saw mills with machines slowly ended local crafts and the old craftsmen died out after the war. The woods were clear felled during the lean pre-war years when estates were hard-pressed to keep going. After the war, good money could be made from shooting, and grants given for clearing woods. University-trained managers had no knowledge or patience with coppice workers and woods once used to make many local necessities fell into disuse. From being a local character, the coppice craftsman became a rarity.

There was a time when a shilling (5p) per day was all a farm worker could expect, one and six (7p) for a skilled horseman or shepherd, and that was for a ten hour day of hard monotonous work. For craftsmen, the material was costly, often paid for in harvest work on the estate, or for faggots for the bread oven. Whilst the wage was low, it paid to have hand-made goods to save expensive machines. Once labour became costly and materials cheap, it paid to buy machines. Once gate hurdles were all hand cleft and assembled; now I can buy machine-made hurdles made from imported wood cheaper than I can make them. So another craft dies out. Wattle hurdles cannot be machine made, and

A coppice wood.

so they sell but only in threes and fours for garden fences. Conservation means the woods are no longer available for me to work in, even a good worker with good hazel would be hard-pressed to earn even a minimum wage for very hard work. The number of remaining craftsmen in Bedfordshire can be counted on one hand.'

DONALD STEWART

The Draper

Although the first purpose-built department store appeared in London in 1877, this form of retail organisation was very rare, and, in villages and larger communities throughout the country, the traditional range of shops continued to trade unhindered until well into the twentieth century. Such shops were family concerns, offering employment through several generations of each family. Customers were served personally in a relaxed atmosphere where requirements could be discussed and advice offered. Friendly conversation was the order of the day. Customers were, after all, friends and acquaintances. If the customer's requirement could not be met, then the retailer would normally undertake to obtain the required item. 'The customer is always right', goes the adage, and the shopkeeper would be courteous, always prepared to serve, with no apparent time constraint, and very eager to please. The shop was a part of the community, as was the retailer, who after all had a reputation to safeguard. A business depended upon its reputation within the local community, and traders were proud of their established reputation.

Traditional shopping is all about relationships between customer and retailer, quality and service – good advice, good quality products, excellent service. This was personalised shopping, where the business bonded with the community. The small trader cared for his business, for his community, and for any staff he employed. Although community shops may have offered only the bare necessities, they satisfied the needs of the community. Compare this form of retailing with modern-day shopping! Present-day retail giants offer a wide range of standard goods, displayed in the most impersonal of surroundings. Shop Assistants are difficult to find in these plastic palaces, but if the question is ever posed 'have you got . . .' the answer is always ' if it's not there we haven't got it'! Profitability seems the priority, not customer satisfaction. This is non-communicative, de-humanised retailing on a vast scale. The British tradition of public service, and things built to last, has almost disappeared. The customer has become a consumer, encouraged to buy goods which are designed for a short life – built-in obsolescence is the term. Few shops have retained their character and standard of service. The village shop, in particular, was almost a social centre in bygone times – a place to gossip and exchange ideas, keep in touch, enjoy a joke, share a problem. A place where you could sit and take your time. Shop-keepers rarely took a holiday, delivered personally to the local elderly, gave advice and maintained a social link within the community. The shop was a life-line in a sense.

'I was born in 1913 at the first shop which my family owned, in High Street North, Dunstable, near the corner of George Street. My father, Charles Moore, bought this business in 1908, when the stock was valued at £100.

In 1917 we moved to 21 High Street South which belonged to the Tibbett family who had been long established in the town, and was known as "Paris House". Mr Gordon Tibbett ran half the shop as a jewellers and his wife the other, as a high-class costumier.

We acquired No. 23 when Boots the Chemists moved to the Quadrant in the 1960s. These premises had been in the Tibbett family since the middle of the last century and traded as a large Stationery and Fancy Goods Shop. They were also Printers and Publishers producing an excellent Dunstable

Moore's the Drapers, High Street South, Dunstable, photographed in the 1950s. The shop interior has retained its character to this day.

Directory and Guide, starting the Dunstable Chronicle and later very greatly expanding into Index Printers who became timetable specialists, which included producing the world-famous ABC Air Guide.

A point of interest to the writer is that in the early 1850s No. 21 belonged to John Darley, the founder of Methodism in Dunstable, and since then it has always been in Methodist hands.

During my boyhood, of course, there were no "superstores" in the town. Practically all the shops were privately owned and run by the owners very efficiently, supplying all the many varied needs of the local community. A great many of them were dedicated workers in the Methodist Church.

No. 21 which was about four hundred years old in the front part, had become unsafe, partly because during alterations many years ago, one or two main supporting oak beams had been sawn through, and much of it virtually had to be rebuilt *in the late 1950s. No. 23 had developed from three cottages built about three hundred years ago.*

We have always concentrated on the type of business perhaps best described as "Drapers and Outfitters", supplying Women's Wear, Children's Wear and Men's Wear, Fashion Accessories and Household Linens, in the various departments, although the type of stock has of course, altered considerably over the years.

Up to the last war a great deal of material for many purposes was sold by the yard to be made up at home or by dressmakers – dress materials, serges, coatings, curtain materials, curtain nets, sheeting – bleached, unbleached and flannelette and Wincyette – plain and patterned for nightwear. For many years now, we have found that by far the greater demand is for clothing and bed linen made by leading manufacturers and have dropped "piece goods" altogether.

One thing which has changed dramatically since I was a boy is of course, the traffic on the main roads in Dunstable. Now it is non-stop and old photographs show how empty even the High Street was in the early years of the century. Little or no through traffic – very few private cars, no buses and an absence of tradesmen's motor transport and long-distance through traffic – all deliveries were made by horse-drawn vehicles – the bakers' carts, milk floats, coal carts, goods drays from the two stations, groceries in the International Stores' covered wagon, hand carts and carrier cycles. Passengers were met at Church Street Station by the Sugar Loaf Fly.

Wednesdays were always lively, with farmers and many folk coming to the Cattle Market opposite on the Square.

In my boyhood days few people owned a car and the villages were not served by buses. Although some customers used to come in on the carrier's wagonette, mostly people depended on the trades people in Dunstable taking the everyday necessities out to them.

In common with all the drapers in Dunstable, we

A view of High Street North, Dunstable at the turn of the century. Printed by Waterlows, Dunstable, 1905 and issued in a booklet 'Dunstable – a Healthy Bracing Spot in Bedfordshire', with the compliments of the Mayor and Corporation. Photographs by James Field.
Courtesy Mr Eric Baldock.

established "country rounds", and had a large number of loyal customers in the surrounding villages. These customers, and with so many in the town itself, gave real meaning to the term "family business" for we have many we still serve who are the third or fourth generation of our original customers. This can only be done by seeking to maintain a reputation for reliable quality and pleasant service.

   In spite of the growth of the giant multiples, it is heartening to know that so many customers still like to shop at a local family store. It is hoped that the business started by my father and mother so many years ago, continued by my wife and

The Moore family, 1940. Front row: Mr & Mrs Charles Moore, founders of the business 'Moore's', in 1908. In the centre is their youngest son Brian, who married Elaine, daughter of Rev. Norman Barker, Methodist Minister at Toddington, and his wife Nora. Brian became Financial Director and Company Secretary of Flight Refuelling Ltd. Back row: left to right: Raymond, Company Secretary and Cost Accountant at Hayward Tyler & Co Ltd (died in 1944), Geoffrey, CBE, Director and Chairman of Vauxhall Motors and President of the Society of Motor Manufacturers and Traders, Frederick, Chartered Accountant, who joined the family business. Father and four sons were all Methodist Local Preachers.
Photo: Courtesy Mr W Dennis.

myself and now run by our daughter Pauline, will continue to be of service to the community for many years to come.'

FRED T MOORE

The Footman

In the days of horse-drawn carriages, the footman accompanied his employers on their journeys and his primary task was to open and close doors, lower the steps of the carriage and assist the passengers to board – draping a travelling rug over their legs – and to alight. In more recent times, he would travel alongside the chauffeur. He would be in attendance as visitors arrived, assisting them to alight from the carriage. As a servant, the footman could be allocated other tasks under the direction of the butler, his immediate superior. These might include answering the bell, cleaning cutlery and silver, taking care of lamps and candle-holders, waiting at table, and even more menial tasks such as preparing and lighting fires. Very often, the footman stood behind his master's chair in the dining room, being of assistance throughout the meal. If his master travelled by train, the footman would be responsible for obtaining the tickets, taking care of the luggage, and making his master comfortable throughout the journey.

Tall boys were favoured for training as footmen, and often pay was related to height, with the tallest receiving the most generous remuneration. Clothing, meals and accommodation was provided by the employer.

Although footmen may still be glimpsed on ceremonial occasions, accompanying members of the Royal household, with the passing of the horse-drawn vehicle and the servant, the footman has also passed into obscurity.

'My father was born in 1880 and he was a hotelier who lived, in his retirement, at Bushmead House, Tempsford. This was where he met my mother, who was initially his housekeeper. She was considerably younger than my father.

When I left school at fifteen, it was my father's wish that I enter service as a footman. He accompanied me to Bath for an interview at the residence of the Hon. Sir Algernon Cecil, Sion Hill Place, Bath, which was a crescent of five terraced town houses, made of local stone and comprising basement and four storeys, and having a lift. It was built on high ground overlooking the city of Bath, about a mile out of town, fronted by trees. I was to join a team of resident servants comprising cook, Miss Pengally, butler, Mr Allan, maid and gardener, and a Daily Help called Mrs Barnes. My father was very *indignant, after the long journey down there by train, that we were not given a hot meal, but only sandwiches. He was seventy-five at the time. He was also displeased not to be received and interviewed by Sir Algernon himself, but by the butler.*

I was appointed as footman, and took up residence at Sion Hill Place. Sleeping arrangements were that the higher status staff in the household occupied quarters closer to the employer. His room was on the first floor, as was the butler's. My room was on the top floor, along with the maid's. I was taken to London to be kitted out with a footman's uniform, referred to as "livery", which comprised coat and tails, striped waistcoat, winged collared white shirts, and black shoes. In addition, I was provided with ordinary day wear which was a dark suit. The coat and tails was only for entertaining and for special occasions.

I had never been to Bath before and was very taken with the city, and found the architecture fascinating, even at the age of fifteen. My hours of work were long, but I had one afternoon off each week and one evening, and one Sunday every two

John Marshall, footman, in livery.

BEDFORDSHIRE'S YESTERYEARS

weeks. *This was how I spent my time off, wandering around the city alone, sight-seeing.*

Sir Algernon was an elderly, frail gentleman with a pointed Sir Walter Raleigh type beard, who spoke very softly so you could hardly hear him, and had a great economy with words. He spent all of his time in his study, researching and reading. He was a bachelor. The butler used to wait on him, wake him, take him a tray of tea, get out his clothes for the day, help him to dress after a bath. He would go to bed in the afternoon, get up about 4 o'clock and have very small dainty cucumber sandwiches and have dinner later, usually on his own.

The butler used to play tennis nearly every afternoon at a club in Bath, while Sir Algernon took his afternoon rest. During his absence I would be on duty and dreaded the telephone ringing, as I would have to take a message. "This is the Hon. Algernon Cecil's residence" I would stutter into the mouthpiece. After I had finally established who was speaking they would ask to speak to Mr Cecil who was usually not available, and then would come "Is Allan there?", in an abrupt, impatient manner. "He is playing tennis" I would say apologetically . . . Needless to say, I nearly always got the name of the caller, or the message wrong. In those days people of note didn't have a lot of time, patience or respect when talking to "servants".

On other occasions one of the bells in the servants' hall would ring and you would look up to the swinging flag of the room in question, and set off, not knowing what to expect when you got there. All the other staff would be resting or on their afternoon out, and this was another nightmare of my early days.

The butler was having his wicked way with the ladies at the tennis club, and was in the habit of returning to tell me explicitly about his antics. He seemed to have a fetish with white lacy knickers! I've been a tennis enthusiast ever since! He had a butler's Sitting Room and his hobby was making tapestries, and he would spend time alone there doing this work.

I assisted the butler and waited on tables in his absence, when Sir Algernon had guests for dinner. When I first went there I had no idea what a finger bowl was used for. A finger bowl is a medium-sized glass dish with a small amount of water, which was placed on the left-hand side of the table setting. The wine glasses were placed on the right. The finger bowl was used when certain things were on the menu, i.e. asparagus and, of course, fresh fruit. Fingers would then be dipped in the finger bowl and wiped on the serviette.

Another of my tasks was to clean the silver. I was also taught ten or twelve ways of folding a serviette, but I could never remember more than two or three. Laying the table was difficult, and an exercise in precision. Knives, forks, wine glasses had to be placed in precisely the right place in relation to the diner. It was not uncommon to have a rule and measure off wine glasses and silverwear from the edge of the table. The centrepiece of flowers and greenery was usually picked from the garden in the summertime and took a long time to arrange.

Sometimes the maid and myself and the butler were in attendance, standing near the sideboard, ready to clear away and serve the next course. We had to wait until everyone had finished eating before doing so. Sir Algernon would give a very slight nod of the head in my direction, which meant the crockery could be cleared away and the next course served.

When walking downstairs to the basement or to the butler's pantry, I would hastily thrust into my mouth any delicacies left on the serving dishes before cook's beady eyes alighted on them and she had the same idea. When Sir Algernon was on his own one of his favourite dishes would be cheese soufflé or something very light. He was not a large eater. There was a serving lift on a pulley, which was pulled up to the height of the dining room from the kitchen. I usually found it quicker to nip downstairs. Everything was served on a silver salver (small tray), from a glass of water to letters and newspapers.

One of my duties in the wintertime, around four o'clock in the afternoon, would be to go around the ground floor of the house shutting and barring the internal wooden shutters. Stoking the boiler in the basement was also one of my duties and I remember the sulphurous fumes would get on my chest and I would come out coughing and spluttering, but this had to be done several times a day. It was actually the gardener's duty but he would often be away doing other things, which meant I was left to attend to this. On odd occasions the boiler even went out, and it was quite a nightmare re-lighting it, before the house became too cold.

For a boy of my age, it was a depressing scene, an elderly man creeping about the house all day. It was a lonely life and I had no friends there, no one of my own age. It was not a happy time of my life, far from it. I think my father was disappointed when I left, but not altogether surprised.'

JOHN MARSHALL

The Forester

Forestry involved maintenance of woodland, thinning and felling, re-planting, coppicing, bark-stripping and so on. Wood is always in demand, in particular in the construction industry. Wood is selected for particular uses; for example, elm has damp-proof qualities and was traditionally used for coffins, ships' timbers and in the construction of quays and such like. Oak is a tough wood, and has been used for centuries in the construction of buildings, homes and barns. To overcome the problem of rising damp, oak timbers were used with the stump-end upwards! Pine was ideal for pit props, scaffolding and construction, and willow, which is also water-proof, has been used, among other things, for boat paddles, propellers – and, of course, in the manufacture of cricket bats.

Woodland maintenance was a physically-demanding task, but an essential part of estate management.

'I worked on the Woburn estate all my life, forty-seven years, and thirty-eight of that was forestry. I went there as a boy leaving school and joined up with the others when I first went in the park [Woburn]. I was road boy, and 'ad to clean up the 'orse muck each day and sling it across the grass, ya know. And then when you'd been on that job for about eighteen months they'd put you out with the men in the park, working with the men. Forestry followed during the war. Wartime came and they took so many of us out to go in the Forestry Department and then when we 'ad done war-time, I carried on the Forestry, that was out in the woods on pit propping for the mines, on what they called the "big stuff" like ya see in that photograph. In them days, after the war a normal day could be leaf-raking, clearing the rides of windfalls: any roads were blocked with trees, that 'ad come down, you 'ad to go and do 'em. I used to go on 'edge cutting as well, in them days with Chris's brother [Ralph Creamer].

There 'ad to be two load a day put on the rail else there was bother with the 'ead forester. 'E 'ad to carry out two truck

Arthur and Ernest Peacock carting firewood with horses, just after the war.

loads a day on the rail. One time they wan'ed us to work all night but the foreman we'd got said "no". 'E said "when the men 'ave been 'ere all day carrying trees about, they don't want to do it at night as well". That stopped that ya know.

During the war the routine was fallin' smaller trees and cutting 'em up for pit props. That was when you got on your 'ands and knees. You cleared that. Two men 'ad what you called a range each, if there was enough men. Sometimes they'd be three. Used to cut the trees up with a bow saw, eight inches to a foot stuff. Used to fall 'em with a cross-cut mostly. They all 'ad to be carried out so as they could be picked up by the vehicle. That went on every day, day after day, hour after hour. What you see on the estate now, most of it was felled in the war. We 'ad so long, so many of us, pit propping and when they were starting planting, we 'ad to go on that. You planted others as you felled the trees, planted as saplings, after the war, about a foot 'igh. They're about twenty feet now.

You 'ad to cut 'em up where they was, in lengths that they'd got to be, anything from two foot six inches to eight feet. Then they was carried out to the ride and put into sizes. You started an 'eap for those sizes so when you got out there you knew which one to drop it on. Then two lorries a day took 'em to Ern Peacock. 'E was the 'ead 'orse keeper: Ampthill Station, or Woburn Sands Station, mostly. Scotch pine, Corsican pine, Spruce (that's ya Christmas tree). Most of that was planted about forty years before cutting. Now it is all planted up again, in the same trees. When they was setting these little trees they 'ad to dig the 'ole by 'and. They called 'em plants, not trees. I used to grow thousands of 'em in later years, when the war finished. I ran the forestry nursery.

In the war time there was twenty or thirty working. When I first went there it was eighty, and there was eighty in the park as well, and they 'ad always got a job to do. A lot of the men 'ad to go in the army. I didn't pass for the army so I didn't go. I was only Grade 4. In the 1914 war Canadians were felling the wood during the war period. Two of 'em stayed on after

Jack Tyler and Dennis Cripps carting firewood by lorry.

the war but they've passed on now – Reg Smith from Eversholt – 'e dropped down dead in Bedford – and another who lived up Jackdaw 'ill. I 'ave got an idea they were in the army and were brought 'ere to do that work. Lumberjacks they were.

There were acres and acres of woodland, in different size lots. One piece might 'ave forty acres, others twenty acres maybe. One on the way to Evershalt 'ad one 'undred acres. They 'ad different names: Palmer Shrubs, Milton Wood, Arnold's 'ook, Cuckoo Spinney, 'unger 'ill, Aspley 'eath – it was Aspley 'eath where they were in bulk – Aspley 'eath was all forestry and there must 'ave been two or three 'undred acres in there. An' that's only one side of the estate. Bracken Fields, Millbrook side, Steppeney Wood, Flitwick Plantation, that's all fir trees, and still is now. Bracken (fern) – most woods have got bracken in 'em – sweet chestnut, 'orse chestnut, the one you play conkers with, there was oak – perdunculator one was called! The 'ead forester, Parker, 'e'd say you 'ave got to plant up for the next forester, two 'undred years ahead, to do any good.

Ron Inge and Joe Showler carting legwood with adapted tractor and trailer.

We felled a big tree at Aspley 'eath at one time, about thirty years ago, felled it by cross-cut, not chainsaw. Used to be on ya 'ands and knees with a cross-cut and ya knees used to get so sore ya daren't kneel down! Used to be three men one end and one the other. It only cut one way, only cut when you pulled it to ya. It was curved like a blackberry briar. That was Bow Brickhill. We brought it out, as best we could, with the 'orses. They came with a timber carriage with two 'orses and we loaded it on to the carriage and got between the gateway, and the carriage broke into two pieces. The tree 'ad to stop on the ground and everywhere was blocked up. It 'ad to stop there for two or three days while we got something bigger to move it. Then they come with a forestry tractor to move it.

Mr Frank Mitchell was the 'ead forester when I started. 'E used to keep us on our toes. The day they buried 'im, well we all lined up at the Park Farm office, the majority of men on the estate went. Four or six of our fellows carried 'im out the 'ouse and just as we got outside the door there was an 'ell of a flash and bang of thunder, and someone said "they're fighting

114

Arthur bark peeling.

*now to see who's gonna 'ave 'im". 'E went on a timber carriage
to Woburn. 'E 'ad been there since 'e was a boy, and 'is father
before 'im. They cut a lot of laurels which was all tied down
each side of the carriage and up the middle so 'is coffin stood
on it, so you couldn't see the wheels when it went round, but
just the green leaves of the laurels. 'E was buried up in
Woburn Churchyard. This was after the Duchess
disappeared.*

*We used to 'ave to ride a bike up to Little Brickhill and get
there at 'alf past six. I've been at Woburn Sands Road when it
struck six, and then got to bike down to Back Wood for half
past six. You were knocked up before you got there! He'd stand
there and look at 'is watch when you arrived [Frank Mitchell].
Then you got a telling off.*

*I've worked in all of them woods in my time, worked all
over the estate in my lifetime. Buttermilk Wood, all conifers,
Circuits Cover, Back Wood, 'orsemoor 'ills, Chorl Wood,
Aspley Wood, Millbrook Woods, a lot of that is pine, Maulden
Wood, which was sold.*

*I've been a shooting man all my life and still shoot. I shot
through the war, even though you could only get about five
cartridges at a time. I used to send some to London – pigeons:
my butcher placed 'em in cold storage. Used to get a cheque
Wednesday morning as regular as clockwork. They went to
Central Market, London. They 'ad 'ares and rabbits. This was
forty years ago. Now you can sell 'em to butchers. Even a fish
man buys wood pigeons, fishmongers, at 89p each, ready for
the oven. Flitwick Market I've seen 'em recently.*

*I can remember well over thirty years ago starlings
sometimes came in flocks to roost, and I 'ave shot as many as
fifty or sixty cartridges a night. They do make a mess – kill
the trees. they don't bother about starlings now. Wiseman was
in charge of the estate then. They paid us overtime every night
for doing it.'*

ARTHUR SEDGEWICK

*Lord Andrew's Christening celebration bonfire, Woburn Park,
1960s. The forestry workers had been busy bundling up faggots of
spruce and scotch pine for the bonfire for several weeks before the
event, the Christening celebrations for the present marquess, Lord
Tavistock. In the centre is the head forester, Mr Rowlands, and to
his left is Arthur. The event was staged in the park, for a private
celebration, to which all staff were invited.*
Photo: Courtesy Bedfordshire Times.

The Grocer

With the coming of the supermarkets, many traditional shop-keepers and trades people have disappeared. The grocer's business was a thriving one years ago, stocking all manner of things from cheeses and cooked meats to toiletries and cigarettes and tobacco. Many products were sold loose, and weighed to order before being wrapped. The customer waited at the counter while the grocer fetched the items required, all in rather a leisurely fashion, whilst chatting about families and local events. For anyone who wished, groceries could be delivered, usually for no extra charge. It was customary for orders to be phoned through to the shop, the goods being recorded in each customer's individual order book, then boxed and delivered by the errand boy on his tradesman's bicycle, and paid for at the end of the week.

'My father, Edmund Charles Bourne, was born in December 1882, and married my mother, Ethel Laura Hulford, both from Plumstead, in 1909. They came to Dunstable in 1919

Bourne Bros., Grocers, High Street North, Dunstable, in the late 1920s.

with my sister Eileen, and my father's twin brother and his wife, and bought a grocer's shop in High Street North, more or less halfway between Union Street and Clifton Road, Dunstable, which is now trading as a video shop. Until four years ago, it had continued to be a grocer's shop. The house itself must have been built around 1905. The business was known as Bourne Bros, and my father retained the name when his brother and sister-in-law returned to London, but eventually changed it to E C Bourne in 1932.

My father was a family grocer, who served the community in that area, the High Street itself, the back streets and side streets. It was a real community, in those days when tradesmen generally lived over and behind their shops. They had a valued set of customers who would place their order over the telephone – the old black pedestal telephone in the hall – and he would make it up in the evening after the shop closed. The errand boy would then take the shop bike with the wicker baskets on, the next day, and deliver orders to the far flung corners of Dunstable. Customers tended to stick to brand names like Hartley's Jam and if you took the wrong thing you would have to change it. It was very much about serving the community. The shop was close to Waterlow's, the big printing firm, with 1,500 employees, on the one side, and so they picked up some of the Waterlow trade. The Grammar School was a hundred yards away on the other side and the boarders at the school used to come across for things for their tea. He didn't make a lot of money, and had to work very hard all through his life, but it was a very happy home and both my sister and myself had a sound and caring upbringing.

My father belonged to the Methodist Church on the Square and gave up his time to that very generously. He was a Trustee of the Methodist Church, a Society and Circuit Steward, a very loyal man. Sunday was the sabbath in those days, a day of rest and relaxation and going to church, so I wasn't allowed to play ball games outside on Sundays. He had a great love of nature, and was knowledgeable on *butterflies and moths, in particular. He was interested in sport, a member of the Literary Society, and played bowls. He had a wide circle of acquaintances and people liked coming into his shop. He had a good sense of humour and was very honest, and people would come in and ask his advice as well as coming in for their goods. Some would pop in every day for a pound of butter or two pounds of sugar, for example. It was not like taking a trolley round the stores. It was a family grocery and he sold to families. My mother helped insofar as emergencies were concerned, but otherwise did not work in the shop, as there was an assistant. She helped in the sense that she was always a considerable backup and support and used to make mince pies at Christmas for sale in the shop. They were noted for the ham which they cooked and baked, and their bacon. So she did an awful lot behind the scenes, and looked after the house. My recollections date from about 1927.*

From the pavement, there was a stone step up into the shop, with a small window on one side and a large window on the other side, and there was a door which opened and clanged a bell at the top. There was a fanlight over the door and a blind with an acorn knob, and product advertisements stuck on the glass door. The large window he would make up every fortnight, in the evening, or on Thursday, which was early closing day, and the little window he would make up once a month, and change the contents. Inside the shop the floor was wooden, and also the ceiling, from which electric lights hung down. A part of the ceiling came down in the shop at one time, but it was in the evening fortunately, and was cleared up at great speed.

On the lefthand side as one entered, was the provision counter and on the righthand side the grocery counter, and towards the back of the shop there was a cross-section of shelves which linked the grocery counter with the provision counter, and they were very much display shelves and very often had dummy goods cartons on them. These display shelves really came to life at Christmas, with special displays.

Behind the provision counter which went down the lefthand side, that's where all the bacon, cheese, lard and butter was served – all the fats – and he had one of those old red and white bacon slicing machines which cut the bacon and ham to the width that the customer wanted. There was a pair of scales close to that, where the lard and cheese were weighed. He would cut the lard with a knife and put it on a piece of provision paper and weigh it on the scales, similarly the cheese, which was initially cut with a cheese wire from a big round cheese drum which used to be kept outside. On this counter was the working area, and further down, displayed on it, there would be a basket of eggs. Seniors' and Shippams' Pastes, Bovril, Oxo, etc.

Behind the counter against the wall there were big wooden shelves coming all the way down, where produce was stacked, and that's where the soups and tinned fruit and fish were neatly arranged – all the Heinz, Crosse & Blackwell, Oxtail soups, Mulligatawny soups and things like that. Further down, there would be other produce that the shop would stock, like suet and sauces. At the back, going out left, there was a door leading out into the yard, which we always called the "yard door", and just to the right of that there were kept dog and cat foods, also drawers of prunes and dried fruits.

On the grocery counter side on the right as you entered, that was much more a serving area so orders would be made up on there, when customers came in for weekly groceries. Behind that, more wooden shelves with all the jams, jellies, blancmanges, cocoa, chocolates, Bournvita, packets of tea, custard powders and items of that nature. All the sugar and flour was stored there. Very much the grocery side. There were a couple of small shelves where he stocked a small selection of cigarettes and sweets, toothpaste, Brilliantine. Below the wooden shelves there was a whole row of drawers going all the way along, about thirty small drawers in which were stored all sorts of things customers wanted, like nutmegs, Aspros, powders, essences, cough sweets, angelica, all the little things. According to which drawer you opened you would get a lovely scent coming out of them. If you opened the right drawer it was like smelling the spices from the big ships coming from the Orients. It was magic. He also stored some of his own materials such as the order books. They went the whole length, and then there were more shelves below that and below the counter where there were whitening material and soaps, Reckitts Blue Bags, things to do with washing and scullery work. Balls of whiting, and starch. Along further, near the window, there was also a coffee machine which ground coffee.

Behind the big window there were half length green drapes and the goods in the window were priced with cards which my father printed. Behind, in the shop itself, was a biscuit rack, hinged, which one of the biscuit firms had given and although there were also biscuit tins on the floor, the rack, which swung open, contained square large tins of biscuits – Peek Frean's, Huntley & Palmer's, McVitie's, Crawford's, Jacob's, all the big names.

Behind the cross section of shelves was the till, and there was another dimly lit counter which backed on to the stairs where there was the "house door". Below this counter were four very big large shelves and there was another weighing machine on this counter, and these large shelves had Demerara sugar, soft brown sugar, haricot beans and butter beans. They would be made up in blue cartridge paper and weighed on the scales at the back. Also on that counter at the back there were two or three old cannister tins filled with "Shag" (bits and pieces), and elderly men would come in early in the morning and ask for "a penn'th of Shag, please". He would weigh it out on a small sliver of paper, and pass it over. It was generally smoked in a pipe, low grade tobacco. Nearby there were shoe polishes and other types of polish.

In the central area of the shop where customers came in and stood, or sat, as there was a little old chair in one corner, there were also some sacks of corn and seed and open dog biscuits, and if it was dry, two of three of the sacks would be put on the step outside, as you went into the shop.

There was wood everywhere, floor, ceiling, shelves, counters. There was a slab of marble on the provision counter. At the back of the provision counter where the butter and fats were stored was a marble slab, and further down the counter there was marble, to keep it cool. It was a very homely shop with a lot of character and my father, every morning, would sprinkle the floor with water from a can and sweep the floor down so it was clean, and two or three times a week he would wash the pavement outside the shop so it was clean for people to walk on. Tradesmen did this all over the town. Once or twice a day a man came along to sweep the gutters too.

Outside the yard door was a lean-to and a sideway and as you went down the sideway on the left were crates and boxes of tinned fruit, etc., stored for bringing into the shop. Under the lean-to there was always a vinegar barrel which had to be rolled down to the shop from sheds at the end of the garden. The barrels had a tap and a bung from which it was poured into a tin mug, a bottle or a customer's container. The shop bike was put in the lean-to and empty boxes ready to go back to the delivery firms.

Then there was the house itself, tall and long, going down the side at the back, past the lounge, hall, living room and scullery, and then two warehouses, lower and upper, joined by a wooden flight of open steps where there was stored a lot of material that had to be stored under dry conditions, under cover, but was not needed immediately in the shop. Flour, and crates would be taken down there, bottles of this, that and the other. There was a very big pair of scales which you could stand on. There were racks in the top warehouse on which we stored apples from the trees in the garden, and other things.

My father opened the shop at 8.00 in the morning and closed it at 6.00 o'clock, a bit later possibly on Saturday. He closed between 1.00 and 2.00, as did most of the tradesmen in the town and Thursday afternoon was early closing day. All

Edmund Charles Bourne, the grocer.

the shops observed that except the odd cafés. It was a regulation, to compensate for Saturday working. He worked in the evenings, doing the books and making up orders. When the war years came all the coupons had to be counted and it was difficult to find an assistant then.

We had an errand boy, a series of them, and mother came in at one time and served, but her job was really doing all the cooking and keeping the rambling house clean and tidy.

My parents made a gorgeous garden at the back, just a few yards off the Watling Street, which was absolutely full of all sort, of flowers. Bushes and shrubs, a wild place with bracken, pathways, a summer house which they gave each other for their silver wedding anniversary, sunken garden, birdbaths, swing, winding paths. They loved being out there Thursday afternoon and in summer evenings, any time the weather was fine. It was a marvellous place to play in and grow up and full of wildlife.

Our customers came from all walks of life. We had a lot of travellers from various firms coming in and who stayed for a number of years with the same firms, and father got to know the travellers and vice versa, very well, and they seemed to like coming into the shop. You would have people coming in for five minutes for an odd item and others for an order and others who would want to stop and talk.

At Christmas we used to sell non-alcoholic bottles of raisin, ginger and orange wine, and the shelves were full of

Christmas goodies and crackers. Once somebody bought a bottle and came back afterwards complaining about the flavour and father checked and found they were alcoholic! It was obviously a mistake. At great speed all the bottles were taken out and the wholesaler was rung up and they were substituted. He could have been in real trouble if the customer had not mentioned it. He was a teetotaller.

I was helping once, as a small boy, taking bottles into the warehouses. I dropped one and it smashed and father said "Oh dear, there goes my profit". All profit from that item lost through one smashed bottle of non-alcoholic wine!

We never had problems with contaminated food. There was an official who came from Bedford to check the scales to make sure no-one was cheating. He used to come feeling under the scales. My father took exception to this, to think that someone might suspect him of cheating.

No-one made any fuss in those days. He was always very pleased when he got a new customer. If someone moved away that was a loss of a customer. It was always a fine balance of profit and loss. He would get anything that a customer asked for, even though it might mean half a dozen items of the product left over, because the customer then decided no further ones were wanted. He ordered from the representative of the firms. Sometimes deliveries would be left on the pavement and might be there for a couple of hours until someone had time to bring the goods in. No-one touched them. Everything was delivered to him, he didn't have to go and buy it.

My father was about thirty-seven when he started the business, and he retired from the business in 1949. He was virtually a one-man band during the war, and sold out after the war. Mr T A Cowper bought it as a going concern, under very amicable circumstances, and modernised the shop a little. His speciality was cheeses, as father's was ham and bacon.

My father died in 1967.' COLIN BOURNE

(A full account of Colin Bourne's boyhood can be found in 'Bourne and Bred'
– The Book Castle.)

The maxim of our business is 'service'.
Our purpose is to supply reliable goods at fair
    competitive prices.
'Quality first' is our aim always; inferiority never
    stands the test of time.
Cause for complaint we try to avoid; anything amiss
    we are anxious to hear of.
Upon your confidence depends the stability of our
    business; to retain this is our first objective.

(From the 1930s Order Book of
E C Bourne, Family Grocer,
131 High Street North, Dunstable.)

The Hedger and Ditcher

A hedge is a fence of bushes or low trees, usually planted to divide land, or act as a wind-break. The earliest recording of hedge-planting in this country is 940, but hedges have existed for far longer than this. It is estimated that during the Enclosures, 200,000 miles of hedges were planted, and between 1945 and 1985 over twenty-five per cent of the country's remaining hedgerows were destroyed. After the Enclosures Acts in the eighteenth century, boundary banks, formed as ditches were dug to mark boundaries and soil banked up on the land nearest the side of the divide, came to be planted with bushes, often hawthorne and blackthorn, but also other saplings removed from woodland and common grazing areas. The owners' sub-divided plots of land would be separated by merely planting bushes on the flat ground, without the need for a ditch.

In order to ensure that animals did not force a passage through the hedging plants and escape, hedges came to be cut and laid diagonally. By weaving the natural growth between stakes, the hedge becomes impenetrable to stock.

In modern times, hedges serve the same purposes as they did so many years ago, but conservationists also recommend that a properly maintained hedgerow provides a safe haven for wildlife and the hedge prevents soil erosion. The hedge also provides shelter from strong winds. Hedge laying is seasonal work, usually carried out from October to March.

The hedger's protective clothing included knee-pads, leather gloves, gaiters and boots, and his tools included well-honed slasher, axe, hammer or mallet and billhook. After checking the hedge and removing any debris with a slasher, side shoots are removed from the selected stems so the hedge is thinned and ready to be laid. The next task is to cut through the stem of the plants at a forty-five degree angle, about three inches above the ground level, and the stems can then be bent without breaking, so that growth is sustained, and twisted between stakes. In time bark will grow over the cut and new shoots intertwine to form a dense and secure hedgerow. The cut stems are referred to as pleachers. As the stem is bent over, the hedger uses his axe at the point of cutting, in order to bend the pleacher. Once bent to the required height, the remaining stump below the cut, can be removed with a billhook or axe. In bending the pleachers, the brush, or twiggy ends of the stems, are kept to the back. Where gaps appear in the hedge, driftwood which was removed when clearing out the hedge prior to commencing laying, can be used as pleachers, to bridge the gap. Stakes can then be driven into the ground through the stems and in alignment, a short distance back from the hedgeline. Once a length of stems has been laid in this way, lengths of binders (or 'hethers') which are usually pieces of heather, willow or ash, are bound around the stakes and around each other in order to keep the pleachers in position. Once this is done, the stakes can be cut down so as to be level, with the binding. The hedge can be trimmed immediately it has been laid, by using a hook or shears. Remaining debris is finally burnt off.

The final step in the process is to clear the ditch, using spades, forks and grasshooks.

The art of hedge laying survives: evidence of traditional hedging across Dunstable Downs.

A hedger might complete about ten yards in the space of five hours.

'They didn't dig ditches and set 'edges for fun years ago: there was a method in their madness. In years gone by, the majority of fields as we know 'em belonged to different people, and the 'edges were set between fields. I doubt it I was twenty when I started 'edging, and the first bit I did by myself was alongside an orchard, a boundary 'edge. The threshing machine was there and the old blokes 'ad got a fire at the corner of the orchard, to 'ave their breakfast, and they was on about this piece of 'edge, ya see. They says 'whoever did it', they says, 'made a damned good job o' that'. I watched the old folk doing it, ya see. You learnt more by watching people work than you did if you asked questions. You learned as you went. 'Edging is best done in the winter time, after Christmas, when the sap begins to rise.

We weren't 'edging all the year round, but we 'ad always got a job to do on the farm, but nowadays there is no 'edging, no ditching to be done, no threshing. Did I enjoy doing it? Well, any job you do, if you make a good job of it, it gives you satisfaction. It's not a lonely occupation when you've got 'orses to talk to. Per'aps there would be three or four of you ploughing one field. 'Edging, you mostly work alone. You work all day. Yes, oh yes, start in the mornin', stop for breakfast and lunch and keep on 'til time to come 'ome at night. Got nobody to talk to. When you're busy the time goes. It's when you are 'anging about doing nothing when time 'angs. I worked for different tenant farmers. I done a bit for Syratt at Centre Farm, Battlesden, and Randel, 'Ill Farm, Battlesden, and I done some at Leys Farm, Milton Bryan, Mr Little.

When you was 'edging you wore a leather apron, if you'd got one, or used to 'ave an old bag tied around you. You've got to 'ave sharp tools to work with. You can be sharpening your tools right through the day when they get a bit blunt. Used whetstone (some call 'em rub-stones, some carborundram, which was round or square). Used to work in all weathers, unless it rained too 'ard. You'd need a good pair o' gloves, sharp tools and a bill 'ook for your 'edging. You cleaned the bottom of your 'edge out and left your stumps all clean cut so as it didn't 'old the water when it rained. The job needs doing every five or six years. 'Ow do you clear a ditch? You slope the sides down ya see, and what you shovel up you put as soils around your 'edge, which encourages growth, which they don't want today. we 'ad to clear a ditch out prop'ly. Once I worked for Mr Little and 'e wan'ed the water in this ditch to run the other way to what it used to. I 'ad to get this water running up 'ill! A bloomin good depth it was. I more or less managed it. 'Ad to dig it three foot or more to get it flowing the other way. The other end I 'ad only just got to shovel a little bit out. Just 'ad a spade to do that. Why did 'e want it flowing the other way? I don't know, I'm sure. There was a drain in the end of the ditch and it ran down two fields of the neighbouring farm and out at the bottom. 'E didn't want that. 'E said "We'll get that water to come this other way". I was by myself that day. That was not much of a job on your own. You was paid as part of your regular wage, not piece rate, oh no. It all come with your day's work.'

CHRIS CREAMER

A hedge recently cut with a mechanical flail.

The Ironmonger

Goldings, in High Street, Bedford, is one very traditional shop, established in 1867, and which must be known to and used by every local resident at one time or another. It is one of the remaining shops where one can ask for assistance and advice, and where one can buy from an enormous range of goods, precisely as many items as are required, since everything is sold loose.

Screws, picture hangers, key rings, curtain hooks, tools, kitchenware, enamelware, coal scuttles, pots and pans, electrical goods, clothes lines, fly swatters, dusters, door mats, yard brooms, bungalow baths, light bulbs, ironing boards, measures, nuts and bolts. You name it, they sell it! As for galvanised bungalow baths, the last one was sold about five years ago, to someone without a bathroom. Now they are more likely to be used for bathing large dogs, or mixing cement.

'I came to work at Goldings sixty-seven years ago, in 1925, and at that time we had a blacksmith's forge here, with the blacksmith operating from the rear of the premises. We were ironmongers, and this was associated with the work of the blacksmith. We used to repair many things then, including pots and pans and kettles. You would fit a new bottom after removing the old one. You didn't throw things away because they developed a leak. Now it's a throw-away society. We had a workshop then and used to do plumbing and repairs in and around Bedford. We had a good old-fashioned tinsmith. We made galvanised coal hods which were used with the an-

Goldings, Ironmongers, High Street, Bedford, trading since 1867.

thracite stoves, to feed in the fuel. We also made things for the big houses including baking tins, fourteen inches and sixteen inches square, and all manner of things. We used to patch the bottom of the coal hods and after a few years of use, virtually all that would remain of the original were the handles on each side! People were more thrifty and nothing was thrown away. We did a lot of plumbing work. We had the first gas boiler in Bedford to heat the shop. Before that it was anthracite stoves or paraffin stoves. Central heating was a new concept. We had the first Ideal gas boiler in Bedford, and it is still working. We had a new inside fitted because of the North Sea gas but the outside casing is made of real enamel and is original.

We have used the space we have at the shop to the best advantage, but obviously we cannot extend. Our model department is where the blacksmith's forge used to be. I think originally the blacksmith traded from that part of the premises and this was a private house. We still have the original fireplaces here, in all the upstairs rooms, and we still have some of the original wallpaper on the walls! No-one has lived on the premises in my time here, and we have utilised the space to best advantage. Mr Golding took over in 1867, and the business has been known as Goldings ever since, although the owners have changed. The upstairs lounge would have been used for afternoon tea originally. This is our office now.

Our heating system was installed just before the second world war. We had paraffin stoves standing in the middle of the shop before then. There was no strip lighting, but bulbs everywhere, all over the place. Now there is an inspection once a year, of anything electrical – key cutting equipment and so on. This is safer, a wise precaution. You don't want hazards from loose wiring laying about. I always say we're in business to manage things, not to grumble, that's my motto. We welcome inspections.

It's interesting how times change, like the term ironmongery being changed to hardware: we have to move with the times.

Even the old National Federation of Ironmongers have changed their title to The British Hardware Trade Association. I've got an article here which will interest you, written in 1843 and advising on how shop assistants should conduct themselves. They called those the "good old days": sanctimonious humbug, that's how I'd describe it. Just read the old list of shop rules.

OLD LIST OF SHOP RULES
TO BE OBSERVED BY ALL PERSONS IN THE EMPLOY OF WM. FONTAINE

1st. Honesty. Be very careful in observing the golden rule of the gospel, "Do ye unto others as ye would that they should do unto you," if you were in their position and they in yours; and not only let this be your conduct to your employer, but to every person, rich or poor, customers or fellow-servants, those above or those beneath you in station, for such is the will of your Father who is in Heaven.

2nd. Be very punctual in your attendance on the public worship of GOD. As free men, attend the ministry of your own choice; and leave others the enjoyment of the same LIBERTY, for religion is a matter between MAN and his MAKER alone; therefore seek as much as possible for counsel and instruction from that pure word of TRUTH the BIBLE, and in all things let that BOOK be your guide.

3rd. The shopmen who are single are not permitted to entertain company, and the shopmen who are married are to avoid having friends during the six business days of the week, and as far as possible avoid having children in the shop.

4th. No shopman to leave his home at night for any purpose, without first having obtained leave in writing; and when such leave is secured, then to return not later than half-past eleven o'clock.

5th. The young people living at the Factory are to ask leave whenever they want to go out at night after work is done, or at any other time, and to be at home again at nine o'clock for supper, or at ten o'clock if they sup out. The same time to be observed on Sunday evenings.

6th. No person boarding in the house to be permitted to

purchase drink or food at their own expense; any extra nourishment or stimulant that may be required will be given on application to the foreman.

7th. No drunkenness, profane swearing, or any other evil practice allowed under any pretence whatever. No talebearing or quarrelling permitted.

8th. Each shopman is to keep an account of all payments made by them for rent, taxes, and gas, and of all rents received by them from lodgers in connection with the house under their charge.

9th. The shops to be opened at half past seven o'clock, and closed at ten o'clock precisely, except Saturday night, then twelve o'clock.

10th. The young men and lads at the Factory are to begin at six o'clock in the morning, and leave off at eight o'clock at night.

August 25, 1843.

WM. FONTAINE.
LONDON.

The trouble was that there were no trade unions for shop assistants in those day. I was born in 1903 and Mrs Pankhurst was active at that time, promoting the rights of women. The suffragette movement was successful to a point, but even when women got the vote, it was only for women of thirty and over. They were still discriminated against.

I was apprenticed at Randalls Ironmongers. We worked from 8–1pm, you didn't stop for tea or anything, then 2–6pm you worked on. Even now I don't stop in the middle of the morning for a cup of tea, the others do and I don't object to that, but I don't stop. We weren't paid much but then we weren't worth much. We weren't of much use to our employers. We knew nothing when we started. We weren't worth more than five shillings a week. We have had some splendid schoolboys here over the past twenty years. They are well-educated. They come on Saturdays and in the holidays and are a great help to us. On the other side of the business

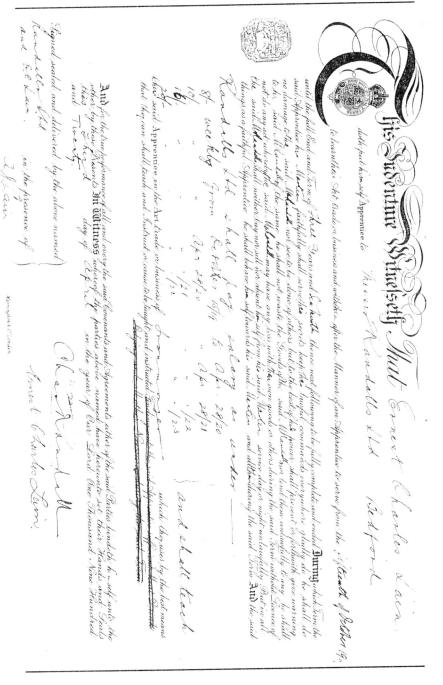

we frequently cannot get trained staff. We prefer women of mature age rather than young people. We have always got on well with the 50-plus staff, and we advertise for mature staff. They do five sessions morning or afternoon and we get some charming people. Two have been here for over thirty years already, two have been here over ten years, the ladies that is. We have older men who start about fifty-five or sixty. They are still fit and can carry on well after retirement age. They love coming to work. Some of the ladies are widows and they like to get out of the house. Every woman knows the difference between a saucepan and kettle and it doesn't take long to pick up the trade in the domestic side.

I can recall that fifty or so years ago people ran an account for everything and never paid on the nail. Some were nice service people and others were not so polite. A lot of people in the Saints district of Bedford came here to educate their children and they were used to having servants. A servant's life could be a hard one, but after the war, and particularly when Woolworths opened, that changed. I remember saying to one lady "when you get Woolworths here your servants will leave and go there". There were three domestic agencies in Bedford for domestic staff – servants. There's not one now, and it is difficult to find daily help. One lady who had been in service said to me that she had Thursday afternoon off and Sunday as well, working at Woolworths. She had never known this before in her life! Woolworths always paid well too.

Yes, many of these wealthy people would come in here, throw their purchases on the counter "book it, deliver it". It was difficult to remember who they were. We'd often book it to several accounts knowing that it would all be sorted out in due course when deliveries were made. Never a "please" or "thank you". There were three ironmongers in the High Street then, and seven within spitting distance of this shop: too many to make a good living from it. In the end, the governor told me to go out on my bicycle and try to get some money in.

We did so much work on credit – even used to clean out kitchen range boilers, because the hard water created work for plumbers. So I'd go around collecting money. People would open the door and say "tradesmen's entrance at the back". I remember on one occasion I replied "I am not going to the back door: I have had a public school education myself, just like your own children, and I won't use the service entrance". The chap was taken aback, but I got the 1/6d which was owing. These people would deal with the big London stores for expensive items, and come to us for oddments. I suggested that we should deal only in cash and not credit, to make the business pay. I thought that we should get some stock in to attract young people too, but most importantly, get rid of the credit accounts. My employer listened and implemented my ideas. It really shook me when he first called me "Mr Lain" in introduction: before that it was always "Lain". There was not much around for young people then. If you didn't join a chapel in those days you couldn't meet a girl. The social life was chapel or church. I suggested my employer should stock models of trains, cars, aeroplanes and get rid of other unprofitable lines

Goldings, photographed in the 1960s.

like water softeners, etc. and at the same time go over to cash. We now have electronics in the model shop and it is an important and large department, popular and profitable. Youngsters come in to buy and older people come with their grandchildren. We have built up goodwill: you couldn't have goodwill with colonels and some of those type of people. The general public are much more polite now, and there isn't any longer that upstairs and downstairs mentality.

We serve if people want to be served. We don't ignore people but don't worry them. I still like chairs in the shop. People laugh and say we have chairs so when the customer hears the price they haven't got so far to fall! I don't think there's any truth in that. We have wooden floors and there is a nice smell of hardware. We like to keep the old image. We have customers who have been here for years and are loyal. We get pleasure out of serving. I could have packed in twenty years ago but I chose not to. I don't serve now because I don't know where the stuff is and what the price is. I do the book-keeping and VAT which I can do and am sensible enough to have professional help where I want it. I get a retired accountant to come in and balance the bank book and he does the wages and every three months looks after the VAT. I do the invoices ledger and all the donkey work, get everything in the book, and get the columns to balance. I can carry on for a long time if I have this professional advice.

Randalls were in St. Mary's Street. They had a lovely shop there which was on the righthand side of the road, beautiful shop. They were tenants and wanted to have their own premises and bought the premises over the road. They then moved the stuff across the road to a brand new shop. I was very pleased to be in the business: I was about seventeen at the time. It was a family business: Major Randall, his brother Charles. I learned a lot about stock-keeping, and how to look after stock. We have stayed small and kept control. Keeping it small has kept it personal. The shop has the disadvantage of being long and narrow and in the week it is impossible to keep open in the lunch hour. On Saturday, when we have extra staff, we keep open all day. You do need ample staff at busy times.

Where would you go in Bedford or Bedfordshire and get three screws? We sell everything loose, screws and nails, and all sorts of things including picture hooks and bath plugs. People like buying the number of things they want. Bulbs come in packs in supermarkets, you can't ask for three or four bulbs of varying wattage, which you can here. In the supermarket you get three or four-bulb packs of the same wattage. We do a lot of key cutting, safe keys, door keys, car keys and so on. Kitchenware is always a strong line, polishes, cleaners, clothes lines, ironing boards, pots and pans. We keep the parts for the things we sell. If the supplier doesn't do spares we won't deal with them. You get as much business from spares as with the main item. Plasticware – bowls, dustpans, linen baskets. Gardening tools.

Our customers like to feel free to look and choose and they like to feel trusted. The more expensive things are in locked cases and knives too because of the danger. We do good business in fireworks in the season. They are kept in glass cases. Brooms and brushes: we have something like 20,000 different things, or so we estimated some years ago. We get valuers in to do the stocktaking now. Three months it used to take me, every night, with the wife's help. It is better to do something productive yourself – there are experts who can do it more efficiently and are more familiar with items and prices. We have always sold thousands of washers for different things, including stone water bottles. A valuer would just look at the amount and estimate their price, not have to count them! They can look and put a figure to it.

We used to deal in paraffin a lot, and deliver it. I used to deliver a two gallon container at 1/10d to a lovely lady in Goldington Avenue. We dealt with them for years.

Mr Golding started this business in 1867 and later sold to Mr Rigby-Smith, about the turn of the century. After the first *world war there were two brothers, one of whom had been an ironmonger in Ilford, and they bought the business about a year after the war ended. The proprietor, Mr Flower, was the person to whom I applied for my job here. I started on 10 September 1925. Mr Flower eventually retired to Seaton at about the time of the second world war. We were later incorporated and the business is now known as Goldings of Bedford Limited.*

I was born on 28 April 1903 in Bedford. My parents lived in Bradgate Road, and when I married I moved to Richmond Road. Father was a commercial traveller selling chemists' sundries. He travelled by train and worked for Smiths Wholesale Chemists of Norwich, which was where he came from. He thought Bedford a good base from which to operate.

I was the middle one of five children and I attended Bates Elementary School until I was thirteen and then went on to Bedford Modern School for three years. All apprenticeships were advertised at Bates Elementary School, and circulated to those about to leave. I left school at sixteen, during the first world war. During the last term we were sent to work for the local farmers. All our holidays were spent on farms. I worked for five weeks at Shotley, shocking sheaths. We were fed like turkey cocks, worked and played hard. Then we went three weeks potato picking in Lincolnshire – such hard work. We were paid so much a row, and couldn't seem to make any money. We learned from the women, the best way to do it. You place the basket between your legs and scoop in the potatoes. Then we made enough for pocket money.

Dad met me at the station when I returned from Lincolnshire and said he'd got a job for me with Harry Ball, Auctioneers. I was there a year and didn't like it. I wanted to be a professional pianist. My father suggested I should take up a profession, a trade like my brother and make music my hobby, which I did. I was lucky to get the job with Randalls as an apprentice. I went to London for experience, in Kingston on Thames, when I completed my apprenticeship. It was travellers who got you a job in those days. They would get to know you and to appreciate your worth through trading with you, and would let you know of any openings, and recommend you. I earned five pounds a week in London and took half as much in Bedford, but I wanted to return to Bedford after my year in London. I've been a member of the Round Table for years, and then the Rotary Club where I was Secretary for some years, but I decided to pack it up in the end. Never be a passenger, that's another motto of mine!

I drove my car until I was eighty-five. I felt competent and had never had an accident but it seems sensible to have a taxi now. I am collected by taxi each morning and brought to work at 9.30 to work all day. I have some domestic help at home, and help with gardening. I enjoy my work and still play piano every day. It keeps my fingers supple and my brain as well. I play classical music and now have a Steinway grande piano.

I have one son, who works in the business now. I also have three grandchildren and four great grandchildren.

There are three directors in the business, of whom I am one. We also have one full-time Electrical Manager. As for temporary staff, we have four men and two Saturday boys. We have four part-time women and three others, holiday relief work, covering for illness, etc. We have long-serving members of staff and I'm pleased to say that we have always had first-class people here.'

ERNEST CHARLES LAIN

The Leather Trader

Leather has always been greatly in demand in traditional industries such as shoe- and boot-making, saddlery and harness making, glove and luggage manufacture, and in more modern times, for upholstery both in the home and in the automobile trade. Leather is resistant to extremes of temperature, and leather upholstery has been regarded as a status symbol, always used in the production of the Rolls

Royce and other prestige vehicles. Animal skins are washed and then tanned, often by using oak bark.

'I left school at thirteen. It was the August holiday and I would have been fourteen in the October, but the authorities made me return after the holiday and finish my time.

I wanted to join the airforce, and go to Australia, but was frustrated in both attempts. You had to be fifteen for the airforce, which I wasn't, but I nevertheless walked to Sharnbrook and got the train to London to join. I failed because of my eyesight. You needed your parents' consent to go to Australia, and mother wouldn't agree! Instead I started work for Charles Pettit & Co in the leather factory. He was successful in business and built for the village of Harrold, in 1901, the Harrold Institute, which was thirty years before its time. It contained a reading room, refreshment room, games room, a billiard table. Ours was the only village in Bedfordshire to have these facilities at this time, early in the century. It all happened before the library service was available, and daily newspapers. In 1911 he built the Institute Hall for dancing and musical evenings. He did a lot for the school was Chairman of the governors. Harrold House was built for him around 1890. This was situated next to the leather factory. It's quite an imposing place, you know, but would look better set back from the road. But then Pettit was a realist and wouldn't have wanted anything too fancy.

I got on quite well in my job at the factory and suffered no real hardship. I earned about nine shillings a week, which helped a lot with my family. I was straining the leather, which consisted of skins of various types, goat, sheep and so on. It all went into a drum to be dyed, and after that it went through an automatic sort of mangle. The next job was to peg it out on boards, to dry in the open. It was bloody cold in the winter I can tell you. At twenty I was in charge of the straining and was getting on all right. They employed about thirty-five in those days, mostly village people. They were all men, no women were employed in the leather trade then. Some skins came from Australia, about eighty per cent from India. There was always a slight worry about anthrax but I don't know of anything happening around this district.

I started in the leather trade in 1917 and stayed until 1957 and decided there was no future in it. At 27 I was manager of the place and my governor was a wonderful chap towards me. He insisted I send my daughter to Bedford School, which he paid for.

Leather workers: eleven father/son duos. Lol Thew is seated front right.

I have a photograph of eleven sons with their eleven fathers, which was taken at the leather factory where I worked, in 1934, I believe. I am seated in the front on the left.

My father was an "engineer" who got the steam up in the morning for the engine and was a sort of caretaker, so he got a company cottage. When the Union came in 1917 and most of the employees joined the Union, it brought well-needed reforms. Until then it was mainly Public Holidays taken but people were in effect stood off for these days, they didn't get paid for them. Things altered considerably then, with paid holidays. Hours were gradually reduced from forty-eight hours a week.

Leather was prepared for re-sale in Harrold, rather than for processing. I took some local boys with me and set up the manufacture of leather for George Fensome Leathers Ltd, in Higham Ferrers, a company which had previously bought in from the firm I was with. I worked my way up and eventually became a company director. This was in the 1950s.

Leather became important locally from about 1850 when Thomas Rate came up from Worcester and started tanning leather in the village. It was close to the shoe producing area and the water was good and plentiful and so the trade flourished in this area. Eighty per cent or so of people in other villages were agricultural workers but eighty per cent of the population of Harrold were in leather, with scarcely any unemployment. Of the four factories, only the smallest one survives.

After the second world war the Indian government decided rather than export the leather in that condition, they would process it themselves. We never thought it would happen but it has, and we are seeing a decline in the leather industry. Bermondsey used to be the centre of the leather trade in London. Rushden is still a shoe-manufacturing town, but firms there buy closed uppers now, where the upper part of the shoe has been made in India and these are attached to the sole, instead of making the complete process. Yeovil and Worcester used to be the centre of the glove industry; our leather was coarser than this fine cut leather.

I still do the buying and selecting for my firm. I have never been to India, as the firm buy from agents, with a contract stipulating standards. My Managing Director has been there, but not me. I would like to have gone when I was younger. I have never been to Australia either, but have been on holidays abroad.

In 1983 I joined the Open University to study for a degree. I was awarded an F for my first unit of work but things did improve! Then my wife fell ill with cancer and I devoted most of my time to caring for her. She came from Olney originally, and she was given an Irish crochet lace collar about fifty years ago, which I would like to see donated to the Lace Museum at Olney one day. This is a lovely example of country handicraft: it belonged to Charlie Cockings, a local man, and it was made by his grandmother. It's well over a hundred years old.

According to the parish records, the Thew family have lived in Harrold for at least three hundred and fifty years. I have lived in the village all my life. I've served on the Parish Council for thirty-two years. I'm Secretary of the Jolliffe & Mead Charity and a member of the Board of School Managers. For many years I was Secretary, then Captain of the Football Club.

The population of Harrold is the same now as it was in 1880. It has always been a small peaceful village, and I hope that it will always remain so.'

ARTHUR THEW

The Market Gardener

Commercial fruit and vegetable growing, known as market gardening, has been carried out in the fertile areas of Bedfordshire, along the greensand ridge for several hundred years. Demand for produce expanded during war times and also in keeping with demand from growing populations in towns and cities, and the coming of the railways facilitated transportation to London and the industrial Midlands, and boosted trade and production.

'My father, John Woodward, was born at Upper Caldecote in 1861. He attended Biggleswade British School until ten, when he began work for Mr Dillimore of Hatch, at fourpence a day, including Sundays. During his later employment with

Mr B Arnsby of Ickwell he gained experience in dealing with horses and attended many horse fairs. He went on to become horsekeeper to Lady Dalton at Upper Caldecote. Whilst in her employ he assisted with the carting of bricks and gravel from Sandy to Old Warden for the building of the mansion (for the Shuttleworth family). Something like fifty horses and carts were plying this route daily, whilst building was in progress. At the age of thirty he bought some land and commenced market gardening in Upper Caldecote, and moved to Maulden in 1921.

My parents were married on 20 December 1881, my mother being Elizabeth Milton from Northill, Caldecote. They raised eight children. I was born in 1905.

I left school at the age of twelve, to help my father on the farm, and this was during the first world war.

I myself, began market gardening in Maulden in 1922, with seven acres. My first crop of potatoes sold for £1 a ton. By 1947 my acreage had increased to two thousand acres. Even during the slump between the wars, business was good, as lorries were then used to deliver to markets in areas of greater population density, and to supply direct to retailers. Several of my

Arthur Woodward photographed in 1951.

relatives farmed in this area.

Much of the land in these parts was owned by the Duke of Bedford, and most farms in the area were tenanted. At one time much of his land holding was sold off: there were six thirty-acres smallholdings in the Green End area and others in Silsoe Road. These smallholdings were offered to local people with an advance of £250 repayable over a forty year period at three per cent. I rented my farm from my cousin, who bought it as a smallholding from the Duke in 1911. After a few years I bought it. The Duke did a wonderful job for this area. From 1927–1983 I worked the farm, and when my wife and I retired we had a property built on part of the land in Green End.

My crops included sprouts and potatoes (my father was one of the first to grow sprouts, known as "buttons", on a large scale in Bedfordshire), parsnips, cabbage, cauliflower, onions, carrots, sugar beet, corn and other market-garden produce. I exhibited at County Shows, and judged at others. My hobby has been the showing of Clydesdale horses at Royal and other leading shows. I've also been engaged in bullock and pig rearing. The animals provided the necessary manure for our crop-growing.

In my time in Maulden I have been a County Councillor, President of the Maulden branch of the Conservative Association, and Chairman of the Maulden branch of the National Farmers Union. As Chairman of the Show Committee my duties have included receiving the Queen, the Queen Mother, and other VIPs.'

ARTHUR J WOODWARD

The Miller

The word 'cereal' is derived from the Roman 'Ceres', Goddess of the Earth, since the Romans believed that grains were provided by Ceres. Grains and cereals have been farmed by man since the Stone Age, and today, wheat is one of the most important grain crops, since half of the world's population relies on it as a staple food.

Since the Middle Ages, white flour has been regarded as purer and therefore superior to that containing 'impurities'. Therefore, during the milling process the outer layers of bran and much of the wheatgerm content were removed, leaving creamy coloured granules which were bleached. Bakers of old are known to have whitened the grain with chalk, alum and in some extreme cases – so it is reputed – arsenic powder and ground up bones! Until relatively recent times, after the bleaching process, vitamins and mineral supplements were added. Fortunately, times have changed, and present-day opinion favours the natural unadulterated product. The natural enzymes present in one hundred per cent wholemeal flour are believed to help the body's natural bacteria to reproduce, thus keeping the body relatively disease-free.

Prior to the time when grain became imported into this country in large quantities – from the USA in particular – crop-growing in rural England proceeded in time-honoured

Bedfordshire's thriving mills, in earlier days. Looking across Dunstable Grammar School's cricket ground at the turn of the century. Photo: Courtesy Mr E Baldock.

fashion, supporting rural and rapidly developing urban communities alike. In this region, as elsewhere in the country, most villages contained a mill, and the miller performed an essential function in providing flour, meal and so on.

Even the poorest of folk had the opportunity to glean, and gleans could provide bread for a family over the winter period, supplementing incomes when times were lean.

'My father, William Herbert Jordan, had his own business. He worked in Sandy, Huntingdon, Godmanchester, Potton and Gamlingay, as a miller and corn and coal merchant. My grandfather, William Jordan,

Holme Mills · Biggleswade

Bowling by the windmill in Biggleswade.

milled flour at Holme Mills, near Biggleswade.

There have been mills on this site for centuries. In fact, mention was made of Holme Mills in the Domesday Book. The Jordans acquired the mill in 1855, and at that time there were mills along every stretch of river. In fact there were about four hundred independently owned mills in Bedfordshire then, powered by wind and water. We alone have remained for the past twenty-five years.

Holme Mills is operated by water-power, being located on the Ivel, a tributary of the Ouse. The water wheel which supplied the power was fourteen feet in diameter and made of apple wood. If the water level dropped, then a 20 hp Hornsby-Akroyd engine was used to provide an alternative source of power. There was a time when my grandfather supplied electricity privately to nearby properties, but this came to an end with the advent of television, when the picture would fade if someone down the line switched on an electric fire so reducing the current!

The grinding was originally done using the millstone system, with three pairs of millstones. However, in 1896 the mill was destroyed by fire and was then re-built, becoming one of the most up-to-date of its kind in England. A new Roller System of milling was installed, and this remains today, in its original condition, as a monument to the technologies of a bygone age. It is still in continual use, powered by a Gilbert and Gilkes Water Turbine.

Until 1971 we milled and

Holme Mills.

marketed only white flour but, under the leadership of my son, Bill Jordan, in 1972 the company launched into processing rather than simply milling, and produced a completely new range of wholefood flours and processed food products. We also supply Bran and Wheatgerm to the Health Food Trade.

My great grandfather farmed at Tythe Farm, St. Neots and North Bedfordshire, prior to the 1800s. They did haulage contracting for millers and then took over Eaton Socon Mill and also Holme Mills from Powers, who owned several mills. They rented Holme Mills from 1845 and bought it about thirty years later. I used to come over on Sundays, as a boy, swimming in the river. My grandfather was a very harsh man, but a good businessman all the same. He wasn't averse to sacking people on the spot if the job wasn't done properly. Sometimes he'd sack the whole shift. On one occasion he discovered specks in the flour which neither the Miller nor

Packer had noticed, so he sacked the whole shift. Included was a chap named Bright who was a Labourer (a loader and sweeper, etc.). Bright had worked for my grandfather for about seventeen years. My grandfather said to him "I want you out of that cottage tomorrow Bright". "Where shall I put my furniture, Sir?" Bright replied, and the answer: "Burn it – get it out". I overheard this and had a terrific row with my grandfather, who sacked me as well! My grandfather was a Conservative: no wonder the Socialists were swelling their

Near Biggleswade.

ranks. I was Socialist for years after that incident.

Grandfather was a member of the Biggleswade Conservative Club and Chairman at the time of his death. He was also a prominent Freemason mason for many years and a member of the Bedfordshire Agricultural Society. He had three sons and two daughters, and founded the business with his eldest son, my father, in 1880. I myself later became a partner in the business. Grandfather was a very energetic, shrewd and hard-working man, who continued to

As corn imports grew, so milling facilities became located near the docks, and many local mills became obsolete, (Thurleigh Windmill)).

work, and drove himself to markets, virtually to the time of his death on 11 February 1947, at the age of ninety-three.

After being sacked from the business, I joined the RAF (in 1940). I was recruited, and trained, as a pilot. After 1942 I worked for the ATA and then a short time for BOAC, and went on to do aerial crop spraying in California for Fleetways, until 1949 in fact. I returned to the mill after my grandfather's death, at which time I had to purchase it from the executors of my grandmother's estate, since my grandfather had remarried following the death of my grandmother. When I took over there were three people working at the mill, and now there are two hundred and ninety six, working on the site, mostly on packing of cereals and transport. We've moved from a weekly production of 160 tons of flour, to the production of 480 tons of animal feed, 130 tons of breakfast cereals, all in packets, and three million bars. My son has spent a fortune on television advertising! We work seven days a week, and twenty-four hours a day.

I think my grandfather would approve of our achievements!'

JOHN JORDAN

The Nurseryman and Florist

It seems the first nursery in Dunstable was started in 1871, after which Dunstable became a centre for productive nurseries of all sizes, and the industry offered work to a considerable number of local people. Dunstable tomatoes had a reputation for being firm and succulent. Between the wars there were eighteen nurseries in Dunstable, all producing tomatoes for local and other markets, the most remunerative ones being Sheffield and Birmingham. Since the last war, however, the industry has declined as other industries flourished in the town and foreign produce became imported in ever-increasing amounts. The decline was also due, in part, to the demand for land for housing development.

'Five generations of my family have lived in Dunstable, and it was my grandfather, Alfred George Headey, who started our business – A G Headey & Son – in 1895. He had been in partnership with his cousin three years prior to that, in Princes Street. When my grandfather died in 1930, my father, Leslie William Headey, took over. He died when I was twenty,

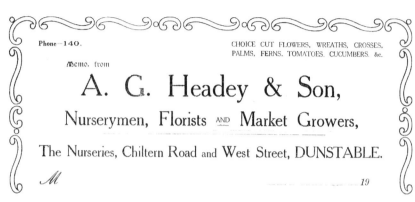

Phone—140.

CHOICE CUT FLOWERS, WREATHS, CROSSES,
PALMS, FERNS, TOMATOES, CUCUMBERS, &c.

Memo. from

A. G. Headey & Son,

Nurserymen, Florists AND Market Growers,

The Nurseries, Chiltern Road and West Street, DUNSTABLE.

M   *19*

and I took over then. I have been the one who has run the business for the longest period, forty-five years in fact. My son Charles worked with me after leaving school and took over completely on my recent retirement.

My grandfather started as a nurseryman and florist, and at that time the nursery side was the larger part of the business. He had an acre of glass in Chiltern Road and Kirby road, and the main thrust was the growing of pot plants, cut flowers, cucumbers and tomatoes. A general nursery one would call it. He used to travel to market in Aylesbury, Watford, and

A Headey's salesman and carter ready for market.

154

Luton, and stand on the markets, in addition to selling from the nursery. He had a salesman and carter who worked for them, and before the first war they would load the cart up with plants and flowers, cucumbers and tomatoes, and set off late afternoon, stop at the pub about half-way to Aylesbury, overnight, and then they would be in the market by about 7.00 the next morning to set up the stall. They would stay there until late afternoon, and get back to Dunstable in the evening. They came home with about £15 if they were lucky, from the sale of goods.

We have always done wreath work and flowers for weddings. It was usually nurserymen who did the floristry trade years ago. Chrysanthemums were the best line in cut flowers as they were fairly hardy types of plants and popular, and could be grown in ten-inch flowerpots, about ten thousand per season, in my time. They would stand outside in the summer and were wheeled into the greenhouses in September. Ferns were also popular, aspidistras, solanums and cyclamen. Chrysanthemums were one of the few winter flowers and were the flowers mainly used in wreaths. During the first war, and the second war, all food, and the production and distribution of tomatoes and cucumbers, were governed by the Ministry of Food and we were allowed to sell so many retail from the nursery and used to have queues at the nursery when they knew we were selling tomatoes.

Things have changed so much in nursery work. Compost is bought in in bags already mixed, from the major suppliers. In 1916 my grandfather bought a six acre field in Whipsnade from which they used to dig the loam for making up the pot composts and were still doing it in 1955. Once back at the nursery it had to be sterilised. They used to make a big heap which stood for six months, chop it down by spade, screen it, and in later times it was sterilised and mixed with peat and fertiliser – about ten operations to produce the compost which you would buy in a bag now!

We have now sold the nursery and are family florists, but I have a wages book for 1938 and it is clear that wages, in real terms, have not changed. At that time, for eight adult men, the wages bill was £20 per week.

There was an acre of land to be dug for planting out hard roots, Canterbury Bells, Sweet Williams, Wallflowers, Forget-me-Nots, which were planted in June time and would be ready for digging up in September, to sell as plants. They were just sold loose, put into boxes and sold by the dozen. It was incredibly labour-intensive. Now people specialise in one crop, they don't do everything as they did in the old days. It is similar with mixed farming. You would have an acre nursery and two men would run it now because everything would be automated. During the war the produce we were not allowed to sell would go to Covent Garden or Birmingham market. The goods were packed in wooden crates. We used to grow up to twenty thousand boxes of bedding plants when we were at our peak, and just after the last war the railway horse and flat cart would come and pick up a hundred and twenty boxes and take them to the station at High Street North and it would just fill the bottom of the railway truck, and they would go off to Birmingham. Later, we used to take six hundred boxes at a time straight to London or Birmingham on the van. We had two men come in and make up the boxes, and we used a lot of old kipper boxes, which we got from the fishmonger. Later we used plastic trays. All the anthracite and coke was brought by horse and cart from the railway in Dunstable. Clinkering out the boilers every morning was the most unpleasant job. It used to be made up twice a day. I remember doing it during the '50s. Nothing changed from the methods used since 1910, until about 1960.

We have done three generations of weddings for some families, grandmother, daughter and granddaughter. They always returned to us for the flowers. In the old days you would have to make a wedding bouquet with a moss handle. Now they are done with an oasis base, which is water-absorbent material, all different shapes, so you don't

88   JAMES TIBBETT'S ALMANACK & DIRECTORY.

have to wire so much. We often provide the bride's bouquet, four bridesmaids' bouquets, headdresses, corsages and button holes. Very occasionally these days we decorate the church with large arrangements on pedestals and pew-end arrangements, and then usually have to decorate the Reception, though that depends upon the type of place. We did one at Ware last summer at a big baronial hall, with a big mantlepiece, minstrels' gallery, table decorations, bouquets, and so on. Bouquets cost up to £80. It was about £700 for doing the whole thing. This type of wedding is becoming less frequent: not too many people go to this extreme.

Although not so frequently now, we do decorate halls for dances and various functions like Mayors' Balls, and that sort of thing. In the '60s when Sir Solly Zuckerman was the big noise at the Zoological Society (Chairman) and was friends with the royal family, they came down at weekends and stayed in the apartments, and we would be asked to make about ten different arrangements, including bathrooms. They stayed in what was the old farm at the zoo, the original farm in the middle of the zoo, completely private. We also did presentation bouquets when royalty visited Dunstable, on certain occasions.

During the '20s and '30s wreaths made up a large proportion of our business. Everybody sent flowers at funerals, because this was a way of showing respect. There would be thirty or forty items for a funeral. In the '50s a good wreath cost fifteen shillings. Now they start at £25. Holly wreaths are still popular for Christmas but between the wars and earlier, every family took a holly wreath and put in on their family grave at Christmas. We used to go and cut holly, then see the farmers and haggle over a price for it. We'd go and collect moss off the Downs and that was a lovely job in frosty weather! We'd rake it up through the long grass. There was plenty of labour and nothing much for them to do at that time of the year.

Nursery work has always been labour-intensive. For

In the early days of the business. Looking towards the Downs, a view of Chiltern Road, then a muddy track, which was covered with all the clinker from the boilers, to help build the road up.

instance, the pots (ten inch pots) were washed and wheelbarrowed into the outer potting shed. Broken bits of pots were put in the bottom of each one, then manure, and then they were passed through to where the men were potting up. As the chrysanthemums grew, they had to be disbudded by hand. You took out all the buds just leaving a centre one. We employed land girls to do this during the war. Cucumbers needed a framework of string so the side shoots could run up them, and then they had to be tied in. Tomato plants had to have all the side shoots taken out. With the potting plants we employed ladies for doing the pricking out. Up to the war all the potting was done by men, but then land girls took over many of the jobs that men used to do. Flowers had to be cut, graded, bunched and packed in wooden boxes for sending to

Blow Downs (named after Thomas Blow, who owned a farm on the Downs), can be seen in the background. The windmill has survived, but is now without its sails.

Alfred George Headey, a founder member of the Dunstable Downs Golf Club. He was also interested in the Dunstable Downs Cricket Club and a great shooting man.

Glasgow. Tulips were also cut and bunched into dozens, not tens as they are now. The tomatoes were graded into sizes and the smaller ones would be sold slightly cheaper. Cucumbers were graded to length.

We used to import daffodils and tulips, hyacinth bulbs from Holland, and they used to be brought into flower early, in January or February time. We have friends in Holland whom we have known for three generations through doing business together. When the cold frames were empty, the bulbs would be set with straw, after the chrysanthemums had been put inside.

Terence's grandparents, his father, and his father's elder brother, Maurice, who was lost in the first world war.

There has been a change in demand over the years. Sadly there are not too many flowers produced in this country now, just a small percentage of what used to be. Much comes from abroad, South America, South Africa, Singapore, because the heating is a great problem here. Because of air transport, it makes it cheaper to import from where they grow naturally. It all goes through the Dutch market. There are about three nurseries in the Spalding area who do most of the growing in this region. One at Biggleswade supplies us with American spray chyrsanthemums grown in Biggleswade. There is a vast choice of flowers from all over the world now. It used to be much more limited.

At present, we have a staff of four and a part-timer. In my grandfather's day he would have made the flowers and wreaths himself. You need about five years of practice and training to become an accomplished florist. Normally we train staff and give college release for floristry courses. Previously it was in-house training. We usually have a junior coming through to train. It is very artistic work, arranging flowers. Dried flowers are a special industry, and we purchase from firms specialising in that type of thing, either locally or imported.

TERENCE HEADEY

The Piano Tuner

Before the days of recorded music and the television – difficult though it is for us to visualise – families made their own entertainment and music, and the piano was to be found in the front parlour of most Victorian and Edwardian homes. Cottage pianos were produced in the late nineteenth century, which were smaller than the standard piano, so as to fit into small cottages, and these played more softly, so as not to cause annoyance to occupiers of adjoining or neighbouring cottages. Popular tunes were purchased as sheet music, and the singing of hymns to the accompaniment of the piano, was a common Sunday ritual, and practiced at other times of the year to celebrate Christian festivals.

In damp or unheated rooms, the piano would soon go 'out-of-tune', especially if not used regularly, and the demand for the piano tuner's services was considerable.

'My father was a painter, glazier and decorator on the Whitbread estate, and that's where I was born in 1913, in Southill. We moved to Cardington when I was about two-and-a-half, and I lived in the village until I met my Gwen, and we married in November 1939.

Alec and Clifford Johnson, young trainees at Frasers.

I left the village school in Cardington in 1927 and started work at Fraser, Son & MacKenzie in Harpur Street, Bedford. Frasers sold pianos, American organs, and repaired and sold all musical instruments, recorded music, record players from the wind-up gramophone to other musical instruments of the day. There was little work at that time and you took the first thing that came along. I went there as errand boy to start with, but after about six months they needed a junior in the workshop and I transferred to there, about the end of 1927 I suppose. I was then apprenticed, at the age of sixteen. That was for five years, and I was

The Bedford Accordion Band, 1938. Alec second from right, and Laurie Alderton, conductor, centre, another employee of Frasers.

taught everything except French polishing. Repairs, rebuilding, maintenance, and tuning, also pipe organ work. I concentrated on pianos and church organ work. We hadn't got a piano at home when I started, but my parents managed to buy one, so I had lessons for about three and a half years to aid my career. I travelled daily on the train to the Northampton shop for the last year of my apprenticeship, to gain experience. I later dropped piano lessons and took up percussion instead. I belonged to the Bedford Accordion Club Band, and ran a small dance band myself for some time.

Once I was trained, I went out to customers, and worked in the workshop, until I was drafted into the Forces. When I started visiting customers, I covered an area in which I could cycle, forty miles or more for five tunings, on many occasions. Cardington to Gravenhurst, Shillington, Shefford, Langford, Biggleswade, Potton, St. Neots. This was my area when I first went on the road. When I acquired a motorbike and sidecar *for pleasure, I was able to extend my area to Hitchin, Letchworth, Stevenage, Huntingdon, Godmanchester. I concentrated on the area in which I already worked. Hardly anyone had transport then. One or two tuners did in the 1930s, but not many. Moving onto four wheels in the early '50s made things even more comfortable.*

The average number of tunings you had to do in a day was five. At Frasers we had to do

Alec playing with his own dance band, 1935.

twenty-seven in the week and if you were short one week, you made it up the next. It was a fixed salary and you adjusted your hours of work accordingly, if you finished early it didn't matter. You would call in the shop to book repairs in or pick up your work for the day, but otherwise you didn't need to come into the shop. You built up your clientele because you were recommended by customers. You were expected to look after your own contracts, and extend it if you could. You had to collect money from the customers and put a schedule in at the end of the week. The office sent bills for people who did not pay personally.

You built up your kit according to the work which you were doing. When we were cycling we were limited to the quantity

Frasers, Harpur Street, Bedford. 1912.
Photo: Courtesy Mr D Markham.

of tools and bits and pieces we could carry on the bike, and any major repair was fetched in by van belonging to the firm. In the last forty years I have carried two or three cases, spare strings, felts and leathers, and extra tools which you don't normally use for tuning. The tool case weighs about sixteen pounds probably, at the moment. Glue, washers, tuning levers, etc., a fairly comprehensive kit. Now it would cost about £500 to kit out from scratch.

During the 1920s and '30s there were five piano shops in Bedford, all involved with tuning, repairing and selling. Also located in this area were up to twenty-five tuners – five employed by Frasers – now in 1995 there are only five tuners based in Bedford, all however, offering full service to their customers.

At Frasers I was involved with pipe organs as well. We were re-building Risely church organ and I made drawings of the *organs. One day a gentleman named De Brisay came and saw my drawings and asked me to do the diagrams and sketches for his book "The Organ and Its Music", which I did. That was published in 1934 and he paid me £5.*

Some of the pianos we tuned were wooden framed pianos. You hardly ever see one now. Professor Richardson in Ampthill had a private collection of pianos and other instruments. "Birdcage" pianos were very primitive. There was one at Blunham. You had to stand on a box to reach the tuning pins. They would be museum pieces now. Church organs were also tuned regularly – I worked on these with Walter Baxter, who was in charge of Frasers' Organ Department.

A normal straight tuning, if the piano is up to pitch, takes about an hour, but if there is raised pitch and if the tuning pins are loose, or anything is split, you are in trouble and that can take up to three hours or may not even tune at all, if too bad. If done regularly, it is about an hour including the time to drink a cup of tea. There was a cottage I visited in Clophill years ago that had a Valour oil cooker which was run by paraffin. The tea she gave me tasted like paraffin, whatever she put the water in was tainted with it, and so was my tea! There was an aspidistra next to the piano and guess what went in there!

The firm's old T Ford wasn't always reliable, and with a heavy piano on board it had to climb Cleat Hill in reverse! Also on one or two occasions we had to hire a "hand cart" from Gravel Lane and deliver a piano in town, by "muscle power".

Still in the '20s and '30s, during this period most tuners wore black jackets and striped trousers and a hat, like morning wear. I got into trouble in the early days of my calling at houses. Mr Fraser stopped me in the yard at the back of the shop and said could I possible wear my hat when I went to the door. "You can't really be polite unless you can raise your hat to the lady!" I said I hadn't got one and he said

"You look too young, they'll think I have sent a boy", so I grew a moustache, which I still have to this day. I called on one customer in Haynes carrying a Gladston bag, like a doctor. The lady opened the door and rushed me upstairs and I then realised she thought I was the doctor she was expecting, as someone was just about having a baby! Quick disappearing act!

In the early days the biggest problem was damp, cold rooms. The piano was usually in the front room, and frequently in the winter you would have to work with your coat on. People didn't normally heat the front room, except on special occasions when it was used. You had to make sure all the notes were playing. Now central heating can cause splitting in sound boards, etc.; it is almost a bigger problem than the damp and cold. Pitch variation is the main problem because of changes in humidity rather than anything else. Too much or not enough humidity. You can fit a humidifier to control humidity in the room for the sake of the piano. It helps enormously. Some people use a dish of water and stand it in the piano if there is room, and so long as you remember not to move the piano. But humidifiers are made specially for pianos – Hydroseal they're called. They are not electric. At least you don't need to work in cold rooms any more!

Following our marriage, my wife and I had temporary accommodation in Kempston, until six months later I was "called up" and went into the Forces. I was away for six years, and that was the only break in forty years working at Frasers. Very soon I became involved in music in the Forces and for nearly two years I was in the Norfolk Regiment Band. Then two years Fire Service in Birmingham, and finally the Army Fire Service until the end of the war, when I returned to tuning pianos.

Frasers were taken over by Carlows eventually, but I left shortly after, and started on my own, in July 1967. I was already known locally, and it wasn't too difficult for me to go independent. I worked with a colleague of mine, Bill Kreis, who later opened a piano shop in Bromham Road. We were both independent, but helped each other. At first, with the firm closing, it was traumatic and it took a few weeks to get financially sound, but it was the best thing that happened because I was able to build up my round to a considerable extent. I must have had five hundred customers in the heyday.

You used to get children rushing about while you were trying to tune, a vacuum cleaner going, children playing with your tools and sometimes you would have to ask for peace and quiet. Now, of course, it's the telly or CD players. There was a record made years ago, and a copy of it materialised in the stock at Frasers, when they were clearing out, – "The Piano Tuner's Lament". It was a thing of the times.

When my wife became ill in 1989 I had to cut down on the distances I went because I couldn't leave her for too long at a time. Some of my work went to Jim Barham, who had just moved into the area, and my other local colleagues also helped out. Many of my school contracts I handed over. I still maintain the Girls High School and I have tuned these since about 1950. I have about six fair-sized contracts, which is now limited to this one, but they have twenty-three pianos

Alec still tuning at Bedford High School in 1991.

there, so I am not left idle. I tune my "old friend" Ernest Lain's Steinway twice a year, that's one of the better ones I tune [See "The Ironmonger", page 130]. He always used to give me a tipple when I called, but now the drink-drive laws are in force I have to take a little bottle, and have it when I get home. I knew him while I was at Frasers. I used to tune at St. Christophers in Letchworth, a mixed boarding college, and vegetarian. Everyone called each other by the Christian name. Everything was communal and the food was good. Thornton College for girls, near Buckingham, all nuns, and Clarenden School, previously Hawnes School, and Princess Eleanor near Hitchin.

With such a wide range of contacts, over a long period of time, – perhaps forty years – both in these establishments, and a large number of private customers, I've made many friends. I've moved on to tune for my customers' children, and even grandchildren! Many of these friends have been so kind during the last few years, and I value their friendship.'

ALEC WILMOT

The Stockman

A stockman is the owner or keeper of livestock, whose responsibility it is to buy the animals at market, graze and care for them, fatten and then sell them for slaughter or otherwise. It was usual to show particularly good specimens at country shows and county shows, as a healthy animal with a good pedigree would command a high fee, at stud or otherwise. A stockman could be a middle man, buying from one source for transmission and transportation to another, for a quick profit. This trade was particularly brisk during war periods, when there were army contracts to be fulfilled. The person responsible for animals on the farm often had the title 'Stockman'.

'Leighton Fat Stock Market was the best in this area, easily. They used to sell a tremendous lot o' poultry there too. These

Leighton Buzzard Market Place.
Photo: Pub T G Hobbs, Luton and Neighbourhood Illustrated.

*butchers round about that bought any beasts that 'ad took
prizes at Leighton Buzzard, they always used to stick 'em well
in the window to attract trade.*

*Talking about drovers, Bunkers 'ad cattle drovers because
they were big people were the Bunkers. Years ago Groom
Bunker the father, 'e got a big contract for the army. 'E used to
contract for beasts; 'e used to buy 'em right from Scotland,
Ireland and everywhere. 'E 'ad to git so many every week for
the army and his chief drover was a chap named Sharp.*

*Bunker 'ad three cars: 'e 'ad one of these old-fashioned open
tourer Fords, and two saloons but 'e used to 'ate the saloons
'cos 'e was a fella with a big belly and 'e couldn't sit prop'ly in
these saloons, – said 'e couldn't use 'em and tha' he'd rather
'ave an open one. Old Sharp the cattle drover used to 'ave to
drive 'im about so one particular day 'e went to London and
phoned through to Sharp to tell 'im to meet a certain train on
Saturday night. Sharp went to meet this train and somebody
said "ah Sharp, are you after your gov'ner?". Sharp says "yes".*

"Well", he says "I see 'im in Luton two hours ago". Sharp says "are ya sure?". "Yes" 'e says, so o' course back Sharp goes to Hockliffe. So 'is train comes in, and there wan't the taxis in Luton then like there is today, and 'e made enquiries. "O yes, I see Sharp waiting for you two hours ago" says the chap "but 'e was fed up wi' waiting for you and 'e went 'ome". So 'e phones through again and Sharp was the worse for drink so they 'ad to send someone else. Bunker's sister came but she wouldn't come with this open tourer, she come with an open saloon, and 'e went nearly crackers. When 'e got there and found old Sharp asleep 'e says to one of these men, "put 'im in one of them cattle pens" he said "and let 'im sleep there. That's good enough for 'im". And that's what they did do.

There used to be an old chap called Adams. 'E used to keep this farm at one time, and old Adams, well they never thought he'd got ha'penny. He used to go along the Watling Street thrashing acorns down for the pigs and used to drive pigs along and used to feed 'em on acorns. Well, when 'e died 'e left £200,000 and it was a fortune at that time o' the day.'

ERIC THORNE

The Tallyman

Years ago, and in fact up until the 1950s, some long-established stores employed Tallymen, who regularly visited villages and outlying areas, selling goods. Traditionally, the Tallyman has sold goods on credit, so that a customer would describe what he or she wanted and the Tallyman would bring the item (or several items from which to choose) upon his next visit, normally visiting at weekly intervals. The customer would have the cost of the item added to his or her account, and continue to make reasonable weekly payments. Many families would have found it impossible to purchase by any other means. This doorstep service saved the customers a journey to town, and allowed them to buy goods on easy payment terms which they couldn't otherwise afford. Over a period of time, a tradesman could build up a very large clientele and this became a reliable source of income. People used to refer to this method of buying as having things 'on the glad and sorry' – glad to have them and sorry to have to pay for them! Some Tallymen traded in their own right, independently. There was one incident of which the writer heard, where such a trader called on a country customer who had asked for a new jacket. Upon trying it on and knowing that it was a particular size, he remarked that it was too tight, too restricting, and asked for one a size larger. Not being in a position to carry a large stock, the Tallyman changed the size on the jacket label and returned it the following week. The customer checked the size, put the jacket on and remarked how much better the larger size fitted. Working men liked to think of themselves as being 'big men' in times past, and so the Tallyman's trick obviously satisfied the customer's ego! Both parties were satisfied.

'Tallymen were very welcome tradesmen amongst the less well-off of the community, and there were many such people. They allowed easy payments and some would charge a small amount of interest on outstanding accounts, although in the early 1900s this would only be a few coppers on amounts owing of several pounds. Some tallymen didn't charge interest on goods as customers were an asset to those who had their own businesses. Customers who paid a little each week or month provided a regular income to such businesses and regular clients meant they always had a foot in the door and that kept the business ticking over.

Some people would be quite open about dealing with the tallyman because they liked "having goods on the easy" or on the "never-never". This meant that they would always be owing some money, sometimes for years, (although a fairly modest amount), because as soon as a pound or so was paid more goods would be left. So really one was never out of debt.

Others referred to the tallyman as the "outrider" from (so and so) [a business]. The tallyman was a very recognisable character, his transport ranged from foot, cycle or pony cart. One I remember always wore a bowler hat and leather knee length leggings and travelled the roads on foot for weekly grocery orders. Another came for lino, furniture, haberdashery, clothes, etc., collected a little cash, a new order, and cycled away until the next week.

The shoe shop on wheels was a pony and trap, all round the trap was a seat piled high with fifty or so shoe boxes, full of shoes, all shapes, colours and sizes. (The trap was a name given to a small type of cart which was a horse-drawn vehicle, very rarely seen these days.) On wet days the shoes would be covered by a small tarpaulin sheet. No doubt there were many more tallymen around with a great variety of goods to offer.'

WILFRED DENNIS

The Thatcher

Straw has been a convenient material for roofing for centuries, not being replaced in many areas until slate and brick roofing tiles became available – through improved means of transportation – or indeed affordable. During the earlier part of this century, when thatches deteriorated badly, often corrugated metal or sheet asbestos would be placed over the thatch by impoverished landlords, as an inexpensive means of rendering the property water-proof.

A tidy thatch is a joy to see, and adds character to so many country cottages. Thatching of cottages, barns and hay-ricks ensured that the thatcher's services were in high demand. In pre-war and post-war times – times of austerity – thatched roofs were often stripped and tiled, but there are now many people who prefer thatch, and also many cottages which are now listed buildings, and therefore continue to be thatched.

'Thatching has been described as one of the earliest types of roofing right from the earliest settlers. Even the Great Fire of London in 1666 was caused through the thatched roof of a

bakehouse catching fire.

I should like to explain just a little about the thatching itself which seems to be three of four jobs wrapped up into one.

Straw (usually wheat straw), is the most used, this being the most durable and long-lasting of the straws, as well as being the less expensive.

When the straw is being prepared for the roof it has to be shaken out on the ground and slightly wetted; then shaken into a heap and after that pulled from one end of the heap and "yealmed". The yealms are put into a string and tied into bundles known as "bottles", which are then ready to carry up on to the roof for the thatcher to use. This preparation is a back-aching job, for there is no other way of doing this work properly.

Other kinds of material have been, and still are, used for this kind of roofing. First the reeds. These can be found growing on the Broads in Norfolk; in Devonshire; also around lakes, moats, riversides and ponds in other parts of the country. A roof thatched with reeds will last from fifty to one hundred years. Then comes the wheat straw which lasts approximately twenty to thirty years depending on the quality of the straw which in turn depends on the type of harvest weather during the growing season, etc. Thirdly, linseed straw, flax, heather, bracken, grass and even brushwood are used. I believe that some crofters' cottages are still roofed with heather.

It is necessary to use a great amount of woodwork for fixing straw to the roof. This has to be prepared and requires very skilled hands in the preparation, viz the cutting of the rods and pegs, in the olden days called goose-necks. These are like a large wooden hairpin twisted in the middle and pointed at both ends. Many hours are spent cleaving these rods and pegs from hazel sticks, usually cut from a local spinney, wood or forest. It takes five to ten years for a young man to become quick and efficient at this work. What I would call, work on the ground.

Then comes the actual thatching on the roof and this requires a lot of patience. Today not many roofs are thatched without being covered with a small mesh wire netting. This is done to protect the roof from birds and damage by gales. A certain amount of knowledge is required to fix this to the roof expertly. Most of the thatched roofs are different from each other with their gable ends, hips and valleys, dormer and eye-brow windows.

The tools used for thatching a roof with straw today are similar to those employed many years ago. The knave or cradle, is used on the roof to hold the bundles or "bottles" of straw whilst the thatcher puts the yealms on to the roof; a hatchet or hammer to knock the pegs firmly into the roof; a needle for finding the rafters; a rake for raking down the straw after it has been fixed to the roof; a large eaves knife used for cutting off the overhanging straw from the eaves; and a pair of shears to trim off any loose straws. A whetstone, pitchfork, wire cutters and a very sharp pocket knife are also used. It has been said that a spirit level is usually carried in the eye of the thatcher. Strong ladders of varying lengths, specially made, are also necessary, in fact are possibly most important for this work. When a farmer required the clover, hay, or corn stacks, which had been built in his field, to be thatched, my dog would often accompany me. He was quite used to climbing up and down the ladder, and when told, would often bring things on to the roof from the ground. He was also good company and would give warning of anyone approaching.

I ought to mention quite a few things which have been found whilst working on the roof, no doubt the smaller of them being carried there by birds, or thrown by children. Pieces of glass are quite common items, and no doubt these could be the cause of roofs catching fire in hot sunny weather. Jackdaws have been known to enter through bedroom windows and to pick up items of jewellery. This could account for one interesting item which I found – a bracelet made up of silver threepenny pieces. Another unusual find was an old cannon ball weighing no less than ten-and-a-half ounces, buried deeply into the thatch, no doubt a stray shot fired from a cannon in Cromwellian times. After the last war, a piece of shrapnel from one of Hitler's bombs was found, which had penetrated into the thatch, almost causing the roof to catch fire. Other things found have been tools formerly mislaid by the thatcher and some even thatched into the roof – such as shears, needles, stingel and other items.

Apart from the thatching of cottages, there were also the rickyards to be thatched and this lasted well into December. During the winter months there were other jobs to be done such as tree felling, hedge layering, ditching, grave digging, etc. After Christmas the threshing machine would call at the farms and this provided additional work. As the day progressed the cornstacks diminished in size and the straw stacks grew rapidly. The chaff was mixed with chopped swedes and mangel-wurzels, oatmeal and linseed cake for feeding to the cows and the cavings used for litter in the

Ernest Parrott (Reg's father), Reg, centre, and his elder brother at work thatching.

pigstys and cowsheds. All the cutting was done with a sickle and the threshing with a flail.

To the best of my recollections I left school at Easter in 1914 being just over thirteen years old, and started work with my father. At that time my elder brother, George, was assisting him with his work as well. My brother later went into farming and managed eventually to buy his own farm.

When first I worked for my father I was not very big or strong and the job proved to be very hard work. My wages for the first two years were board and lodgings and clothes, and 2d a week spending money. In the winter months my father would leave the thatching and do any other jobs that came along such as tree felling, soot sowing, hedge layering, digging, corn setting with dibs, threshing corn with machines and flail, ditching, grave digging, etc. I well remember helping my father to set a field of horse beans for a farmer with a dib and line. It was on February 14th, St. Valentine's Day when we started to set the beans and when they began to grow, the straight rows down the field were a joy to behold. An old saying in those days was "to put four beans in the hole, one for the pigeon, one for the crow, one to rot and one to grow".

These and other jobs would see us through the cold winter months and then when the warmer weather arrived we would return to thatching again.

It must have been 1917 when my father had a poisoned finger and in the end he was advised to have the finger removed, which he did, and as a result was laid off work for many weeks. This is really when I came into my own as a budding thatcher, there being a great demand from the farmers for me to thatch the roofs of the hay and corn stacks. I very nervously undertook to do this work as I had had very little experience of working on the roofs, but my father when convalescing, would come along and give me his advice.

The work of thatching in the farmers' rickyards would last until well into December. After Christmas, when the threshing machine would call at various farms to thrash the corn, extra help would be needed and we would go and give a hand.

During the first world war many young farm workers left the farms to go into the munitions factory in Bedford, and I decided to go for a short time. I cycled the five miles there and back and worked from 6.00am to 5.30pm, but found factory life unhealthy and restricting and after about six months, went back to work with my father again.

1921 was eventful for me because it was our first year to go thatching in the village of Thurleigh. The old thatcher, who had done most of the work in that area had retired and was drawing the old age pension of ten shillings per week for himself and his wife. We thatched several cottages in the village that year.

Between the two wars, there seemed to be a tendency for the thatched roofs to by dying out. Until recent times there were cottages in some villages with a galvanised iron roof or asbestos put on over the top of the thatch as this is supposed to be cheaper and longer

Reg and his assistant thatching at Thurleigh, 1973.

lasting. Today there is a great demand by people who wish to own a thatched country cottage. City dwellers and towns-people alike are buying up these properties in order to relocate or to spend their holidays and weekends in the quiet of the countryside.'

WALTER 'REG' PARROTT

The Timber Merchant and Forester

The timber merchant supplies wood, in various forms, for particular purposes and trades. For centuries wood has been an important basic raw material used to form the tools of many trades. Consider just some of the many uses of wood, such as firewood, building and construction industry, furniture, garden furniture, railway sleepers, coffin making, carts and waggons, vehicles (trams for example), crates and pallets, telegraph poles, fencing, gates, tools, shed and farm buildings, ladders, barrels and many more uses.

In the timber yard one would expect to find wood in all shapes and sizes – poles, planks, off-cuts, beading, skirting, wood for garden and rustic work, logs. Timber is often stood to dry, as dry wood tends to distort and shrink less in the manufacturing process, is less heavy to transport and machines more easily.

'I was born in 1901 in Southill, on Mr Samuel Whitbread's estate. The sawmills on the estate were run by my father, George Perridge, who came from Silverstone in Northamptonshire originally. I had two sisters. I was brought up on the estate, went to school at Southill until I was thirteen, left when the war started and worked on the farm for a couple of years. There were no men left on the farms at that time, only the old men and boys. I liked to work with horses and helped with ploughing. We used to plough with two horses: o' course we could only turn the plough one way. We had to lift it round one way: we used to tip the plough over on the turn and that used to run round itself. The man used to

George Perridge, Frank's father, with a tree felled in Silsoe, 1935.

set the ridge up the field and us old boys used to had to go round and round it. As they get a wide bit here and a narrow bit there they turn it inwards. You couldn't used to turn the plough, therefore you had to lift it out. We couldn't do that.

Then there was a terrific blizzard on March 28th, 1916 and this was when I started in the timber trade. We used to move the trees off the road with horses. During the blizzard several bullocks were killed after eating yew.

My father was thirty years at Whitbreads. I've got a picture of him with a tree felled in Silsoe. It was taken in 1935. He was working at Whitbread Saw Mill, which was on the estate. When the war was on my father got a job at the Warren but Whitbreads wouldn't let him go. You couldn't change jobs, but when the war finished he started up on his own, in 1920.

I got a job in the Warren. There were two sawmills and they had a hundred and fifty German prisoners working there. After the war I left to work for my father, timber carting with horses. He started his own business. Mr Whitbread sold him the property in 1920. My father bought a lot of trees from Whitbreads: he left there with no bad feeling. He died in 1943 and I came to work in the mill.

Much of the wood was elm. Wood was used for coffin boards, posts, wheels and so on. It was not for building because it was new, not dried. It had to be stacked and took perhaps two years to dry. Posts could be cut and delivered immediately, chiefly oak. We bought limes from Lord Brownlow, of Belton House near Grantham. I recall seeing walnut trees in Wootton churchyard on a visit some years ago. We used to cut railway sleepers and waggon sheetings – that's what they make the railway trucks with. Horses went as far afield as Wales at times, collecting timber.

The Warren was partly field years ago and the Forestry Commission took over. Where oak used to be cut it is mostly connifers now: they're used for pit props. As the original trees were cut down, so they went up. Beech and ash went to Wycombe for furniture; lime to Luton for hat block making. The turning was done in the wood by foot pedal (chair legs). Charcoal used to be made in the woods. During the war it was done in a sort of tin affair. It was used in the gas masks. It had to be hard wood – oak, beech or ash. The War Office arranged for this to be done. The boughs went for charcoal, not the tree itself. Elm was chiefly used for coffin boards – now they use chipboard! We took a lorry load of coffin boards to London about every fortnight. Elm was the cheaper of the two but my dad said these would last longer in the ground. It lasts in the water, too. If airtight, it lasts for ever. The old bridges were built of it and it is still being found in bogs. It was ideal for carving. Shafts were of ash, we used to cut felloes for wheels.

Measurements used to be written in Roman numerals with a race knife. These scribe marks were made at the end of the planks. The scribing would be there for ever.

We've found many things in trees – especially nails. The tree grows round it over a period o' time. There used to be a firing range in the woods and some of the trees were full of bullets, – lead. They'd be coal from the railway trucks and we found a knife in one tree. The metal discolours the wood as well as spoiling the saw as the wood is cut. The barbed wire used to be fastened to trees to keep cattle in, and as the tree grew, the barbed wire became embedded within the trunk.

When I first started we had circular saws, then band saws which were automatic. Circular saws were a wide cut so that band saws meant a saving particularly with coffin boards. There were no chainsaws: cross-cut saws were used to cut down the trees and it was hard work. After the second world war it was necessary to get a licence to buy a chainsaw – in 1943.

Of course, we used the steam engine and burnt the waste to get the steam. We steamed all through the second world war. It was always warm, never a cold job.

One day during the war we had orders to cut nothing but twelve feet by nine by three oak for three weeks: it was a government order. It was used in Poole for barges for the invasion. The wood was collected one morning at 6 o'clock. They had to be stripped and stacked for eighteen months. They paid three-quarters when they were cut, and settled upon collection. Every sawmill had a quota. Everything else had to be left aside while these timbers were cut for this three week period.

One of the lanterns in Ely Cathedral is of

Commemorative cabinet in the Airmen's Chapel, Lincoln Cathedral.

timber which came from Chicksands estate. There were two big main beams, fifty feet long and rough hewn. The dome at Wrest Park, Silsoe, which is open to the public, is of our local timber – I cut the wood for that. Lincoln Cathedral contains a monumental commemoration cabinet in the Airmen's Chapel which holds the Bomber Command Books of Remembrance. We provided the wood for the bookcase from Southill: that was seasoned oak. I went to the Dedication Service in 1952.

In the days when sawing was done by hand, saw pits were normally fourteen feet long and eight feet deep, often brick lined. Using a doubled-handed saw, one sawyer stood above, one below in the pit, pushing and pulling rhythmically, as the blade cut through the trunk.

There are very few sawmills about now. You have to have a permit to fell trees.

I sold the mill when I retired.'

WILLIAM FRANK PERRIDGE

The Travelling Greengrocer

Despite the popularity of the supermarket, there are still mobile greengrocers, and various other mobile traders, who continue to make a living from such a business. The door-to-door trader is a boon for elderly and house-bound people, in particular, who rely on personal delivery of goods. Before the day of the motorcar, and even up until the 1950s, mobile traders were to be found in villages and towns, selling to private and commercial customers. The butcher, the greengrocer, the baker, the fishmonger, the milkman, the grocer – including the Co-op van – were all to be found doing the rounds. Even paraffin was sold off the van by a mobile trader! Personal delivery of goods to the door saved the necessity of travelling by bus to town, shopping and transporting purchases back home by bus. A saving of time and money, particularly welcomed by working women and busy housewives.

'My father, Alfred Dennis, was a tenant farmer at Ruxox Farm, Flitwick, from 1922 to 1938. He rented the farm from the council. He had no milking facilities and used to milk the cows in the field, using a three-legged stool, and then carry his milk from the field to the farmhouse. It didn't go through a cooler, but was strained and put into cans. Each can held about two gallons. He was not just a farmer, but a milkman, and a dairyman, and the following day he would set off with an ordinary man's bike, with a tin can tied around the crossbar and two on the handlebars. He'd go down the hill to Maulden and sell from his cans by the measure, off his bike, pint or half-pint. It was only a penny or twopence a pint then. On one occasion he rode there with his milk and when he got there, fell over with his bike and spilled the lot! He had rest places at intervals in the turf along the bank, where he rested one foot whilst keeping astride his bike. He used to point these out to me when we walked along the lanes.

Years ago people knew the local traders well, everyone was on Christian name terms.

Alfred Dennis, Wilfred's father, with sister Hilda, in Greenfield just below Greenfield Mill, circa 1915.

Wilfred's grandfather, George Millar at Flitwick Mill c. 1905, mucking out with the dung cart, in the cattle yard. The mill was demolished about ten years ago and the land sold for development. Also in the picture is Jim Gulliver, who finished up an old man on the coal cart.

I started off selling bread and got a job when I left school at thirteen-and-a-half, in the local bakery in Clophill. Bread was twopence-farthing a loaf then, and fourpence-ha'penny for a large. You could get thirteen cakes for a shilling. I worked there for two years, doing deliveries, and worked in the baker's shop too. You could buy Players at sixpence for ten then, or a shilling for twenty. After I left the bakery I went back on the land, and my father retired early through ill-health. He went into semi-retirement, gave up the dairy farm but carried on with his four acres of land. In those days I remember him picking brussels sprouts and taking them to the shop for ten shillings and giving it to mother for grocery money. He died in 1958 at the age of seventy-four. My mother lived until 1984 and died just before her 92nd birthday.

At the age of seventeen I was called up for National Service and went for a medical, passed and was going into the Royal Air Force. I asked the officer in charge how long it would be before I was in the RAF and he said "Count three weeks on your fingers and you'll be there". It's been the longest three

Wilfred's father, Alfred, pictured with the cart and only Piebald horse in the area, called Tom. The child on the horse is believed to be Winnie, his eldest daughter. 1920s.

weeks I've known. I'm still waiting to hear!

I was working for about five years with a local market gardener and I would hire his horse by the hour and after a day's work, take the horse and do work on my own land with it, or father's. I gave up my job with the market gardener and took over my father's land eventually, and then I spread my wings and came into the greengrocery work.

It was in the early 1950s that I decided to go on the road. I bought a lorry and a small grocery round, which lasted for about five hours, in Bedford, selling fruit and vegetables door-to-door, on a Friday. For the lorry and the business that cost me £100. I took about £18 a round then. I had got a smallholding of about four acres, rented from the County Council, which had been my father's, and I sold my own produce. Cabbages in old money were sixpence, potatoes two shillings for 7lb or 8lb. Carrots, onions, parsnips were the

Doing the rounds in St. John's Street, Bedford, in the late '50s or early '60s. The customer is Mrs Stephens, who 'always had a cup of tea for you at 4 o'clock on a Friday'. The Bedford van was quite a 'posh outfit' at the time. The boxes on top are empties, after the day's business.

same price for years and years, 6d lb. Apples, the best quality from South Africa, were one and sixpence a pound, and bananas, lemons fourpence or fivepence, oranges eight for two shillings. I bought things from Mr W Crawley of Flitwick, who was a local wholesaler who bought at Covent Garden.

The first Saturday morning that I took the business on the road I took one and sixpence, and sold 1lb of potatoes and 1lb of bananas! Door knocking was hard work. I persevered. When I finished up, I was in Bedford at 7.30 in the morning and left about 5.15 at night. I started opposite South Wing Hospital near the Dewdrop Public House, then Newnham Avenue, Kingsley Road, Beresford Road, Tennyson Road, Russell Avenue, York Street, Pembroke Street, and then Wendover Drive, back into Castle Road, St. Minniver Street and then St. John's Avenue where the station was, then St. John's Street, and Grosvenor Street. I came back and re-loaded the van at about 5.30 then set off for Pulloxhill until about 8 o'clock and then came back and re-loaded, then about 10 o'clock at night it was all ready for Saturday morning, then on to Greenfield, and finish in Flitwick at about 12.30. It built up so much I did Thursday and Tuesday too. I visited the further points in Bedford on Thursday afternoon to save time on Friday. There were quite a lot of vans on the road at that time: I knew four or five. We respected each other and didn't tread on each other's toes. If we were short of produce, we would help each other out.

The people I met and knew at this time were wonderful. When I retired I never had to go back for a penny. I never had anything owing me at all. Remarkable.

I used to not only serve houses, but small boarding houses and small cafés and I remember going into a café at lunchtime on a Tuesday and the proprietor was in a flap and gave me a big tin of catering peas to open, which I did. I sat the tin on the table and she knocked it off as she turned round, and the peas went flying, everywhere. She got down on her hands and knees and scooped them up and said "What the eye don't see the heart don't grieve", and "everyone has to eat a peck o' dirt before they die"!

Another lady I knew, crippled with arthritis and living in St. John's Street, couldn't walk and I took her order back. She gave me a pound note, a very large one, the first kind. I said "This is not legal tender and hasn't been for a long time". I didn't know whether to put it in my bag and say nothing. She said she had more locked away. I thought it was past the time to return them to the bank, and saw the manager and told him about it and he said to bring them in. When I went back and told her the next time she opened a tin which contained £60. She said she had been saving it so she had a good funeral. In those days this was a lot for a funeral! The bank changed it.

My business grew, as though it was a family, because everyone was so friendly and there was always a welcome and people knew exactly what time I would be there. When Safeway came to Bedford things began to change and there was more competition. When we first started there were only small shops. In those days it was mainly stuff off the land, not much was washed or cleaned. One thing I did find, we traders would exchange views and forewarn each other if there was anyone about who wouldn't pay: we'd know in advance whether people were good customers and worth taking on, and if the Weights and Measures people were around, and the Health Inspector. After many years of trading, we had to have hot water on the van, soap and a towel, which I had to put in. We had been trading for years without. It was a sort of vacuum flask which we had fastened to the side of the van. There was always somebody around to check.

I started my rounds in the early 1950s and not many people had transport then. There might be as many as three traders in the street at any one time. People watched and waited for us. You could almost load your vehicle knowing exactly what you would sell. It was all in your head, you knew exactly what you would do, you didn't need a computer. You would knock £100 a week up. Petrol was only 2/3d a gallon. Many people had regular orders and people would leave a basket if they were not going to be in. In those days the money would be in the basket on the doorstep.

One thing which did amaze me, I had been calling on a house for some time. The wife would come to the door and sometimes the husband. I never knew what he did, but he always seemed to be at home. One day he turned up with the minister's collar on and he was the minister of the church in Mill Street, the Howard Congregation. I never knew he was a parson. I had quite a fair spread of middle class people, but the older people, the pensioners who you looked after and did everything for, they would always be there and counted on you going and you could rely on them as much as anything. One thing I remember, one old lady who had just come back from the doctor's – I felt embarrassed at the time – she said "He gave me these tablets and I have had two: they're good for . . ." and I said "Oh, I get that from time to time" She took one tablet out and gave it to me. I thought I could drop it down somewhere but she insisted I took it in front of her, and I didn't know what else I could do. She insisted I had it, and that it would make me better!

I had one or two people working for me part-time, at five shillings an hour. One wouldn't take money but would take the produce instead. One emigrated to Australia, the next one said he wanted seven shillings and sixpence an hour but then he went down with angina. An old chap of eighty came for five shillings an hour, but he dropped down dead in the street! Another chap the same age as me started and he wouldn't take money because he couldn't keep away from booze. He sold me a lot of things which I didn't want, but he wanted drink money. My nephew told me he had died, suddenly: I didn't seem to have much luck with staff. My mother was a very wiry lady. She was picking potatoes up in her eighties and she worked with me. Then I married and my wife came with me. It was during the time on the round when she was expecting, and had to go into South Wing suddenly *one Friday. They kept her in and we lost the baby. We did have a daughter later, I'm glad to say. I was thirty-four when I got married, and my wife is eight years younger than me.*

I retired from my grocery round in 1972 and then took up managerial positions with local supermarkets. I retired a year last October at the age of sixty-five, after fifty-two years of work. I am busy in my retirement, and most of my Sundays are occupied taking services in the Methodist churches. I am a qualified Methodist preacher. I started in 1953 or 1954, and since my retirement I have increased my ministry. I have taken as many as seventeen services in three months last year.

Sadly to say the congregations of today are shrinking and younger people don't follow it up, but my own daughter is a regular attender at church. Sunday is not kept as it used to be and people are drawn away by all kinds of things, leisure centres, supermarkets. Speaking as I would preach, people don't know it but they are missing some of the best things in life. I never shop on Sundays. I like to live my own life so that others might see something different in me. We are not here to judge but to lead, and I do not preach to others how they should conduct their lives.'

WILFRED DENNIS

The Wheelwright and Undertaker

Before the days of mechanised farming, any farmer relied heavily on the services of the wheelwright, as he did the blacksmith and farrier. In addition to maintaining vehicles, and wheels in particular, a wheelwright might also be required to do repairs on the estate, and the wheelwright was usually the local undertaker, making coffins and directing funerals. As farms modernised and the demand for the wheelwright's skills diminished, many turned to more general carpentry and to building.

'I was born in the house in which my grandmother was born and where my parents set up home when they were

married. My father was a carpenter, wheelwright and undertaker. He employed a bricklayer and a labourer. The bricklayer was paid one golden sovereign for a forty-eight hour week and the labourer was paid fifteen shillings. I used to have to work in the mornings before going to school and in the evenings after school and in the winter time the only light we had in the carpenter's shop was a candle. The services of my father were always in great demand. He had a contract with the steward of the Crawley Estate which consisted of farms in the parishes of Thurleigh and Keysoe. There were some brickkiln sand piles at Keysoe which used to supply the bricks, plain tiles and agricultural pipes for the repairs of the farms on the estate. My father supplied the timber, nails, paint and tar. He also used to do work for the tenants of the farms, such as making up mangers and cattle cribs, sheep troughs and pig troughs, and cart repairs.

My father bought me a new tool basket and saw, hammer, pincers and chisels and the first place I went to work with him was Ravensden House for Mr Francis Wythes, a gentleman farmer. He used to come out punctually at nine o'clock, smartly dressed, highly polished shoes and short leggings, done up with laces. he came to the shed where we were working and said "Morning Wildman", and discussed with dad about some fencing and gate repairs he wanted attended to at once, then he noticed me at the back of the shed and said "What's that lad doing here Wildman?". "That's my son" says dad, . . . my, and did I feel important! But Mr Wythes was a very particular man, and would not allow anyone about the place, especially boys, so he says "Send him home, I won't have him here". I could see my father was annoyed but he said "I shan't send him home, he has come here to work and help me. If he goes home, I go too", to which Mr Wythes replied "But what can a lad like that do at your work?". "He has been working for over a year and is quite capable of my jobs", and Mr Wythes could now see that dad was getting very angry so he said "What will you charge for

Abner Wildman (Fred's father), outside 1 Cross End, Thurleigh,
circa 1915. Left to right: Fred, Rosie, Mark, Abner, Edward, Alfred.

250.249.04.   **Local Education Authority for Bedfordshire.**   *Form 22*

LABOUR CERTIFICATE No. 1.

AGE AND EMPLOYMENT.	PROFICIENCY.

I certify that *Frederick W. Wildman*
residing at *Thurleigh*,
was on the *6th* day of *November* 1905, not
less than **twelve** years of age, having been born on the *27th* day
of *August* 1893, as appears by the registrar's
certificate [or the statutory declaration] now produced to me, and has been
shown to the satisfaction of the local authority for this district to be
beneficially employed.

(Signed) *Wm. W. Marks*
Clerk to the above Authority.

I certify that *Frederick W. Wildman*
residing at *Thurleigh*
has received a certificate from *E. G. Colson, Esq.*
one of His Majesty's Inspectors of Schools, that he (or she) has reached
the *5th* Standard.

(Signed) *Frank Spooner*
Director of Education.

Fred's Labour Certificate, issued in 1905, showing that he had
reached the 5th Standard.

him?". "Ninepence a day" said my father in a rather loud voice. Mr Wythes said "I shall not pay, we can do without him". "All right" said my father in a quiet voice, called me to him and said "Fred, pack the tools up, we are going". "Where are you going Wildman?". "Home" said dad, "if you can do without him you will have to do without me. Good day sir" "Wait Wildman" said Mr Wythes, "let him stay for a week and see how he shapes up to the job" and turned round and stalked off round his farm. I breathed a sigh of relief that we were not going home.

During the week I could feel that Mr Wythes was watching me very closely, every time he came to us punctually at nine o'clock, but my father was a crafty old bird and he always set me something to do that I could do fairly well when he came to us. At the end of the week he said to dad "That's a very useful lad of yours Wildman" and the ninepence a day was paid without a murmur. I have never felt so sick since that first day.

My next place of work was at the Bury Farm, Thurleigh, a place that I had looked at from the top of Bury Hill during my schooldays and wondered about the activities going on there. Mending the stable mangers was the first job on the instructions of the horsekeeper, who was king of that domain. Next job was mending the sheep troughs for the shepherd, and then the cattle fence in the yards and the cattle cribs for the stockman. These were also persons of importance. I remember the farmer coming into the yard and talking to dad but never mentioned anything about what we were doing, then the horsekeeper, the shepherd, and stockman came and said to Mr Hawkins "Have you got the key boss, we want our corn" So off goes the trio to the granary. The boss unlocks the door and goes in, then follows the horsekeeper with a sack over his arm, and has his horses' corn measured out to him. Next the stockman for his measured out corn for the cattle. Last and least, the shepherd gets his measured quantity of corn for his sheep. This he puts on his shoulder, walks out of the yard about a mile across the fields with this weight of corn on his shoulder, to feed his sheep in a turnip field.

I helped my father for a time, and was then apprenticed to Thomas Philpot, the village blacksmith. I soon got fed up with that and was then apprenticed to a farmer, at Scald End Farm, affectionately known as "Bushel Breeches", on account of the enormous breeches he wore. There were not articled apprenticeships at the time, just an informal word-of-mouth agreement. Having tired of that, my father told me that I would be working in the family business, which is what I did.

Traditionally, the village carpenter made coffins, and this was part and parcel of the business. I started making coffins at the age of eight or nine, before I left school. Coffins had to be made up as quickly as possible. The body was then coffined and left in the home. Before the hand bier came into use, there used to be four men to carry the coffin from outlying areas or from any house to the church. Before starting their journey of carrying the coffin they had a meal of ham, cheese and a pint of beer to fortify themselves for the task ahead. This was at the house where the body was, the home of the deceased. In later years we had a four-wheeled bier, this was at the instigation of the village blacksmith who opened a fund for subscriptions to purchase it. It had a roof over it and the wheels were four feet in the rear, and two feet on a turntable in the front.

There is a bier in Huntingdon Museum, which came from Sharnbrook, and belonged to the Pacey brothers, funeral directors and builders there. This particular one had four posts, a shaped wooden roof, rollers to roll the coffin on and a peg each end to stop it falling off. There was a bar across the front and a bar across the back and two bearers pulled and the others pushed, or held back if going downhill.

The last time the bier was used in Thurleigh was in 1940, for Ruth Clayton, a girl who died of diptheria at the age of thirteen, and shortly afterwards, her father Joe. People paid a fee for the use of the hand cart and a rent to the person who owned the building where it was stored – "the bier fund". They also paid for the making of the coffin, and the necessary church fees. The coffin would be rested at the lych gates before proceeding into church, so the bearers could get their breath back, as the bearers were obviously fatigued. The tressels used in church were shoulder high then, as the coffin was carried by the bearers on their shoulders and was easier to move at shoulder height.

There were a lot of child funerals then, and very often the vicar would give his fee, for the upkeep of the church, back to the relatives. People probably walked long distances or had a pony and trap and needed to be fortified after one journey and before the return journey, and this is how the funeral feast came about. Families have always got together for weddings and funerals, and it gave people a chance to console the bereaved and to meet long lost relatives. The funeral feast is a personal and private affair and my father and I tried not to get personally involved.

The majority of coffins were made of elm, but some people preferred solid oak and they would stipulate which they wanted. Only farmers could afford oak, which was more expensive. According to financial circumstances, sometimes they were made of poplar. These were all English timbers. We used to buy the trees as they stood, let them stand until the bark dropped off, and then they were probably left for twelve months, and then sawn up into coffin boards. They were stripped, and strips of lathe put across the boards which were scattered with sawdust to absorb moisture. The boards were checked to see that there was not excessive moisture, or they would stain, and periodically they were stood out in the winds, particularly in March, to take up the excess moisture so they would not discolour, or distort. They were stood up by the hedge in Cross End Lane. This prevented them from twisting and discolouring. When you use hand tools there is a physical effort and you don't want moisture. It took two men with a cross-cut saw to cut down the tree. These saws were *five feet or six feet long, and had a handle at each end, and the men kneeled down whilst sawing. The ash trees were cut up into three inch and four inch planks, and incidentally, were cut by a five inch diameter saw, powered by steam engine. It could be a dangerous business. You only got two feet six inches or two feet nine inches above the table, and if the tree was any larger diameter than the saw, it was turned over for two cuts.*

Ash and oak were cut into three inch and four inch planks for making cart shafts and wheels. These shafts and feloes – there were about five or seven on the outside of the wheel, they were cut by pit saw. This was seven feet up from the ground level, and one man used to be underneath to pull the saw down and the other one on top. In clay soils it had to be above the ground or it would fill with water, but in sandy soils it could be a dug out pit. The man underneath got the sawdust down his shirt!

> *". . . the everlasting job of pit-sawing was carried on in the bitter conditions of the saw-pit. This was a rectangular hole dug in the ground outside, under a crude roof which kept off only the worst of the falling snow and rain. Each morning it had to be cleared of any snow that had blown in, before a start could be made. Most of the big log sawing was done by a pair of visiting sawyers who were hired for that purpose. Nevertheless, some pit sawing was done by Jes and Sammy and sometimes I had to take the horrible bottom position where a continuous stream of sawdust descended into one's ears, eyes, nose, throat and mouth, and whence you never dared look up."*

(Thomas Hudson's "Wheelstocks and Ploughshares"
– Tabb House Publishers)

F W Wildman the undertaker, pictured just prior to directing a funeral in the 1930s.

On one occasion my father had to go and see a relative at Bushmead, at the Two Brewers pub. He was away for a few days and came back to do a funeral, which we boys had done the day before. We were only about twelve or thirteen at the time.

The wheelwright side of the business was in constant demand, making and repairing carts for the local farmers. I brought the wheels to the village blacksmith to be "shod", which meant putting the metal tyre on. There was a big metal ring in the blacksmith's yard. We used to measure the wheel with a circular wheel with a nick in it and counted how many times the measure revolved. We then lit a fire on the iron base and it was dropped over the wheel and doused with cold water and then holes were drilled in the tyre and clout nails inserted at intervals, to hold it in position because in the summer time the wood shrank quite a lot. They would last thirty or forty years if done well. There was always business, as horse-drawn carts, traps and so on were the only form of transport then for the majority of people.

The feloes were made of ash, the spokes oak, and the hub elm. These three woods were chosen for reasons of hardness. Elm is not as hard as oak, and ash is not so hard as oak. The spokes had to take the strain of the wheel and if the axle did not fit very well, there was a wobble on the wheel and extra strain on the spokes.

We didn't make furniture commercially but I did make various items of furniture for our home, such as wash trays for laundry work. These were tapered at all angles. Clothes were washed in these wooden tubs in the wash-house and they were then put through the mangle. When my wife and I returned from honeymoon in 1921 I made one for six shillings, and this was all the money we had in the world. We'd been to Great Yarmouth and returned broke.

At one time my two brothers and I were working at Putnoe Farm, beyond Mowsbury, near Mowsbury Park, some considerable distance from Thurleigh. The tools were too heavy for one man to carry and had to be carried on the handlebars of the one bicycle we had. We worked out a plan for getting there in the most expedient way with our load. One rode ahead, having the tool bags on the bike, the others walking. The cyclist would then leave the bike after a certain distance, for the next one to pick up, and walk on. The next cyclist would then repeat the exercise, overtaking his brothers and leaving the bike. And so we leap-frogged our way to the farm arriving with at least some energy to spare!

My father used to ride a penny-farthing and carry the tools on his shoulder. The axe handle went through the tool bag and he had the handle under his chin because two hands were needed to mount a penny-farthing.

On one occasion my father gave a price for work at Keysoe to erecting a large farm building out of cut timbers, cut down and roughed up one side. Another Bedford firm put a price in but didn't get it so called on my dad to jeer at him, calling him a "hedgerow carpenter". He picked the first man up and threw him in the ditch, and the second man, followed by their

CERTIFIED COPY of an ENTRY of BIRTH.

(Issued for the purposes of the Factory and Workshop Act, 1901.)

| Registration District of | _Bedford_ | | | | | | | | |

Sub-District of _Sharnbrook_ in the County of _Bedford_

No.	When and Where born	Name if any	Sex	Name and Surname of Father	Name and Maiden Surname of Mother	Rank or Profession of Father	Signature, Description, and Residence of Informant	When Registered	Signature of Registrar	Baptismal Name, if added after Registration of Birth
199	Twenty seventh August 1893 Thurleigh R.S.D.	Frederick Wallace	Boy	Fred Wildman	Rose Wildman formerly Hardwick	Journeyman Carpenter	Rose Wildman Mother Thurleigh	Eighteenth September 1893	G.B. Snell Registrar	

I hereby certify that the above is a true Copy of an Entry of Birth in a Register Book in my custody.

Witness my hand this _22nd_ day of _October_ 19 02

W.C. Scott

Deputy Superintendent Registrar.

[Note.—The word "Journeyman" to be struck out when the Certificate is given by the Surgeon.]

Fred's Birth Certificate, showing his father's occupation as Journeyman Carpenter.

bicycles. He was a very hard man, my father, very powerful and strong. "Country Cousins" was another derogatory expression used by the town carpenters to describe their rural counterparts.

Funerals averaged about one a month, but it was a small community and I reckon I must have buried twice the population of Thurleigh in my time! I covered the surrounding parishes as well, of course.

My wife did all the clerical work in our business and made the linings for the coffins and the coffin pillows. She was a teacher by profession and taught at Thurleigh School before she married, but women were not encouraged to work after marriage, at that time. She was a scholar and pupil teacher at Thurleigh School.'

FREDERICK WILDMAN

WORKING WOMEN

Working Women

Introduction

Although women, and even children, were employed in large numbers throughout the eighteenth and nineteenth centuries in industrial centres – in the mining and cotton industries in particular – it was less common for women to work in rural areas, and this was the case in Bedfordshire. In many poor families, girls would go into service in large houses or farmhouses, to supplement the family's income and to make room for other members of the family in the cramped conditions of many cottage homes.

A girl entering 'service' would learn the skills necessary to become a useful member of the household servants, and could progress through the ranks, to become Cook, Nanny or House-keeper over a period of time,

First world war poster, encouraging women to join the war effort. Courtesy: The Imperial War Museum.

learning the customs of the gentry, the habits and speech patterns.

Girls of wealthy parents were less committed to work, and taking a 'position' was regarded by some as depriving others with greater need for income. Victorian attitudes tended to prevail: a woman's place was in the home, caring for the breadwinner and raising the family. Some husbands, for reasons of pride, declined to allow their wives to work, as this tended to indicate desperate financial need. Moreover, with large families and housework involving much manual labour, a woman's work in the home was an essential element of family life. However, this all changed with the onset of the first world war, when the call-up created an urgent need for a replacement workforce in industry, munitions and on the land. Duty demanded that women play their role as workers in society.

In 1920 a Government committee set up to report on the employment of women on police duties came to the following conclusion:

'We consider that the experience of the war has proved that women can be employed, with advantage to the community, in the performance of certain police duties which before were exclusively discharged by men ...'

(Bedfordshire Police 1840–1990
A F Richer, Pub Hooley)

Courtesy: The Imperial War Museum.

At last, labour engendered prestige, and the working woman gained respectability. Another step in the process of emancipation for women, which obviously led to both greater economic and social status for women.

The Baker's Assistant

'After leaving school I went to work for Miss Simms at the bakery in North End [Haynes]. I delivered bread by pony and trap, in Stamford and Cotton End, but later delivered by bicycle. Mr Oliver did the baking, and I had to fetch twelve buckets of water each day from the well on the top of the hill, for the bread making. The pump opposite the entrance to Hawnes Park country house, Haynes Church End, was installed by Lord John Thynne in the 1860s. There was no other tap water in the village then, when I started work, and nor was there electricity. I also had to clean out the stable where the pony was kept. On one occasion someone asked me to deliver a letter whilst I was on my rounds, and paid me one penny for doing this, but gave it to my employer to give to me, and he kept it. I had worked there for three-and-a-half years, but mother wouldn't let me return, because they had robbed me of this penny.'

BEATRICE MAY WEBB

The Factory Worker

'I left St. Matthew's School in High Town, Luton when I was fourteen, and was apprenticed in the hat factory, which was the only thing to do in those days. When the war broke out in 1914 I was fifteen. You had the choice of going to the High School for girls, but I went out to work. I enjoyed life you know – used to go to First Aid and helped with the classes. I was always interest in that type of thing. I got married when I was twenty. I still remember the first time he took me home to meet his mother. She'd got a machine in the corner where she did boaters. She was a charming lady.

Tom and I set up home in a little house belonging to a

relation, and you know, the housing problems were just as bad as they are today. He'd been in the Air Force before we married. I really blossomed out after my son was born – always wanted to be doing something. I got in with the St. John's Ambulance Brigade and worked for them for many years. They had a little place in Barbers Lane. They had a Medical Comforts Depot and if people were sick they got a doctor's certificate and we loaned them rubber sheets, back rests, wheelchairs, and things like that, for use at home. I was in charge of that for many years, and then they moved their Headquarters to Williamson Street, and I took charge of this for them. They often arranged outings, and I'd accompany people; recuperation holidays they were.'

ETHEL MAYES

'When I left school there was really nothing but factory work. I started at Marion & Foulgers, off London Road, Bedford, making picture frames, camera parts and so on and stayed there for four years. After that I went to work at Meltis the chocolate manufacturers. There were all English girls there at that time. We worked from 8am to 4pm but there were often more on short-time than on full-time. We had three days on and three days off. We were sometimes paid a "beddow" which was a bonus paid for work which exceeded the targets which were set, and it was normally twelve shillings extra. We did crystallising, packing, and checking. The checkers are now called "supervisors". I used to earn £1 a week, out of which I gave my mother ten shillings, or half. If we became unemployed we could sign on for unemployment money, but I was lucky and stayed there until I got married.'

MABEL HILLYARD

'After my marriage and a short spell of factory work, I took a job in Park Avenue, Bedford, as a Domestic Help. My employer was a Scottish gentleman, Captain Blair DSO, a second world war naval captain who had seen service on

submarines. He had been an Antarctic explorer in his younger days, and was a Director of Dudeney & Johnson. I took care of his treasured model ships on the occasion that he visited his brother in Canada, removing them to my own home until he returned some six months later. Captain Blair was a bachelor and lived alone, and on one occasion I arrived for work only to find that he had suffered a heart attack. From that time onwards until his death in his late seventies, my husband and I cared for him.

My association with Captain Blair spanned some fifteen years. I believe he was Head of Trinity House, which was something to do with lighthouses, was titled, and had an island named after him. He was a regular visitor at the De Parys Club. He was friendly with the Commander of a shipping line, whom I notified of his death, and he arranged for Captain Blair's coffin to be draped with the Union Jack for the service which was held at St. Peter's Church.'

FREDA BROWN

The Hat Maker

The hat trade, and in particular, the straw hat trade, has flourished in the south of the county since the early 1800s, as most plait was made in this and the neighbouring counties of Hertfordshire, Buckinghamshire and Essex. Much work was done by 'out-workers', who could work from home, often assisted by their children. Hat making in Luton and Dunstable in particular, was a major source of income for women.

As the straw hat trade remained largely a domestic industry, many houses had workrooms built at the rear, and established small-scale manufacturing units. Luton's total exports for 1906 were £953,585.

In the early nineteenth century children were taught to plait at home, often as young as four years. Subsequently they were often sent to plaiting schools (known as 'sore thumb schools'). Girls left the plaiting schools when they were old enough to work steadily without constant supervision, after which time they worked at home. Boys were brought up to plaiting as well as girls, until old enough for more suitable employment.

The following is an abstract from an essay read by Mr A Tansley before the Society of Arts in 1860:

> 'Women, who are skilful and quick, earn good wages, and a well ordered family will obtain as much or more by plaiting than the husband who works on the neighbouring farm. The earnings of a good worker will be from 5/- to 7/6d per week in a good state of trade.'
>
> The employment of women in the hat making industry in Bedfordshire was very substantial, and Luton is still renowned for its expertise in the millinery trade, and the industry continues to employ the services of women 'out-workers'.
>
> (Extracts from Luton and Neighbourhood Illustrated,
> Pub. T G Hobbs)

'In my younger days we lived in High Town. Luton was a thriving hat manufacturing town and goods in transit to and from the factories were sent by rail. Trolleys collected the crates and boxes from the factories, and The Great Northern (now Bute Street) kept horses and vans for this purpose. All of George Street, which is now shops, was factories then and the trolleys would be out lining up in the street waiting for the goods. Everywhere was hats, and most of the jobs were in the hat trade.'

ETHEL MAYES

'I have worked as an outdoor and indoor milliner in the hat trade since 1952. As a young girl I served my apprenticeship and learnt all aspects of the trade. Then as a young married mother I was able to work outdoors. This was very convenient, with young children.

'Hat work in the '50s and early '60s was low-paid and I used to carry the hats in boxes back and forth to the factory on the end of the pram, then all the hanging around the factory waiting for more work to carry back home. Best part of the day would then be gone. If no work could be got ready I would have to go home and return the next day.

With young children, it was impossible to sew in the day, so after the children were tucked up in bed, I would start to sew the hats, until sometimes 2 or 3am. At times I would feel so tired that I would do the last few hats wrong and next evening have to undo and re-do them. I never enjoyed ribbon work, band and bow, and up to today I do not like this type of work. Although it was very hard to earn a few pounds at least it was better than nothing and as my husband was a student, every penny helped.

Over the years life for the outdoor milliner has improved. The work is taken to the home and collected when finished. The milliner today has her needle and pins and cotton supplied. Work is now much better paid even to the point that a milliner can work as a self-employed person. Of course, some hat manufacturers are better than others to work for. The higher class of work the higher rate of pay. Myself, I now work twenty hours a week to suit myself, in a hat factory, where I do all the patterns and samples, and also have work at home. I also time the samples, and rate of pay is based on how long a hat takes. As I sew expensive work I am now happy with my life as an outdoor milliner.'

CORAL BANGBOYE – Luton

'At one time it seemed as if everyone in Luton worked in the Hat Trade, until Vauxhall took over. Dyeing the plait (which usually came from Switzerland or China) into a fashionable colour was the first stage. This was a rough job, the men wore large aprons to stop the colours going all over them. The dyeing was done in huge vats. My first job was polishing felt hoods with a felt bob. Each time you had a different colour

211

reckon there were over three hundred small hat manufacturers in Luton in the boom, mostly small like mine, usually extensions attached to the back of a dwelling house. For several years we lived and worked in the same premises in the centre of town.

Outworkers were the mainstay of the trade as the factories could not accommodate many staff and the women liked working at home to look after the children. When I was very young, I recall the women used to walk to the factories with large mysterious black cloth sacks and pick up the materials needed (i.e. bundles of plait and large reels of cotton) to make the hats. They sewed them up on a seventeen guinea or a box machine supplied by the manufacturer. The shapes were then delivered back to the factory, where they were stiffened and blocked into shape; padded and trimmed by the milliners. The finished hats were packed in large wooden crates piled high and loaded onto drays to be taken to Luton station for despatch all over the country. Years later when I had my own factory I remember the luxury of owning my first van, which enabled me to deliver outwork to the ladies, this time for trimming. We packed the hats and materials in long cardboard boxes and went as far as Harlington.

I had previously processed these hats in my factory, dipping the plait hoods in a bowl of stiffening and hanging them by a cotton loop on rods to dry. Felt hoods were steamed over a steam pot and then put onto a blocking machine. Many is the time I had steam burns on my arms, and my wife says she can remember boiling eggs in the steam pot!'

RONALD OVERHILL

The Lacemaker

Lace making was a thriving cottage industry in North Bedfordshire during the 19th century and early 20th century, offering employment to a large number of women home-workers. It was a flourishing cottage industry, enabling women to play their part in contributing to the family income. Before the advent of compulsory education, many children were sent as trainees to lace-making 'schools', commonly known as 'sore thumb schools'. From as young as five years of age, children would be taught the skill of lace-making, whilst at the same time receiving the rudiments of an education. The main object of the exercise was training and the production of a marketable commodity, but there can be do doubt that parents would have been more committed to the teaching and acquisition of skills than of education.

There is no doubt that the lace making schools enabled women to earn and to cope with family responsibilities at the same time. The number of Bedfordshire out-workers in this trade were considerable.

Lace schools were held in cottages and conditions could be unhygienic and cramped, with as many as thirty pupils huddled into 'classes'. They would be seated on benches with three legged stools known as 'the lady', on which rested the pillow, before them. Occasionally children worked two to a pillow, one on each side. There were tuition fees! Frequently in the summer, work would be done outside and it is reputed that the older pupils chatted whilst working, and lace-makers would often sing pop songs of the day – hymns of course.

Rigid discipline would be enforced through physical punishment at all such teaching establishments, and by the age of ten a child would be expected to earn about one-third the amount which an adult would earn. One small local village is said to have had nine lace schools at one time. Hours ranged from five to fifteen hours a day, depending upon age. Eventually legislation and new attitudes to education, put many of the schools out of business.

Lace making came to be taught in Parish and other schools in the lace making areas, and evening lace schools then appeared. Grants were provided for this purpose around the turn of the century, but by 1924 these were suspended.

There is no doubt that the straw hat and lace making trades allowed girls and women to develop as an economic force, in a way that domestic service, hitherto the main employer of women, did not and could not have done.

'Lace-making classes started at Maulden School in 1912. All the local girls learned the skill. We used to spangle our own bobbins, which means putting beads on the end for weight. I have a photograph of my lace-making class, taken when I was about twelve. The teacher on the right in the picture, Miss Mabel Palmer, was learning with the class. The class was taught by Miss Treacher, who is in the centre of the picture. She was the daughter of a Silsoe schoolmaster. I am second from left. This was the first class of its kind in Maulden. We had to buy our own pillow, which was straw-filled and rounded. The village carpenter made the wooden horse to stand the pillow on, with a hoop at the top (I still have mine). The pillows are made flat today, to stand on any table. One of the girls made paper weights, collars, bookmarks and so on from the 1920s right up until the time she died a few years ago – Miss Inskip. She was a teacher and did evening classes.

My mother's grandmother made lace and I still have some of her bobbins, some bone, some wood. We used wooden ones at school.

Lace-making classes was the beginning of a highlight in village life here in Maulden. The class was held once a week, in school, but we brought the horse home during the holiday and made some at home. I made lace for what we called "five o'clocks". They were tray cloths, one yard square. My mother promised a friend one at four shillings, but I was so bored doing it: I reckoned up that I earned half a penny an hour! Interest in lace-making continues in the village and there have been displays at the church from time to time."

BEATRICE WOODWARD

'Each afternoon after school I used to rush home to do pillow lace with my mother. I learned pillow lace making from my mother when I was about eleven. A lot of the women

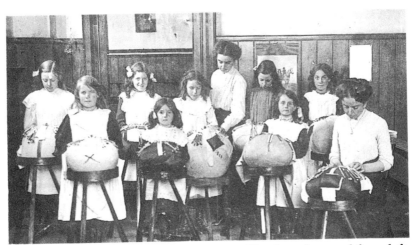

Lacemaking class in Maulden: Beatrice Woodward second from left. 1912.

Lol Thew's wife came from Olney. She was given this Irish lace collar about fifty years ago. which Lol would like to see donated to the Olney Lace Museum one day. This lovely example of country handicraft belonged to Charlie Cockings, a local man, and it was made by his grandmother. Lol believes it to be well over a hundred years old.

used to congregate in one house to make lace, and my mother did this from an early age: she never went to school. May Vincent, my cousin, who lived at Keeley in what is now "Peartree Cottage", then a butcher's shop, collected the local lace and sold it to Braggins in Bedford. She also selected the cottons.'

SARAH HILLS

'Sir Arthur Black, a Member of Parliament and local farmer, owned the lace-making factory in Bedford Road [Wootton]. It was more accurate to describe the work at the factory as "finishing" rather than lace-making, but there were many local cottagers who did lace-making in those days. The factory is now sold and converted to two residential dwellings.'

FREDERICK BURRAWAY

'When I was twelve or thirteen, Sir Arthur Black, MP for South Bedfordshire, had two bungalows built, and my father helped build them. They were originally built as a lace factory. I remember seeing bales of lace which came from Nottingham, and many girls from Wootton and Marston worked there repairing this lace. My sister worked there in fact. This was going for ten years or so. It was then converted into two bungalows.'

STANLEY LOVELL

Lace makers at work in Church Walk, Wootton.
Photo: courtesy Mr W Juffs.

The Ladies' Hairdresser

'When I left school there were apprenticeships, and this was the only way to a decent job. I paid a premium down to learn hairdressing. This was not my first choice of career, as it was my ambition to become a Physical Culture mistress. However, I had friends in the hairdressing business and they were an influence on me at this time.

My first job was at Hawkins in Mill Street, Bedford, where I learned to be an "improver". In later years I became a partner in Fowlers, in Upper George Street, Luton, and after my marriage, took a temporary position in Salon Barry's in Bromham Road, Bedford.

Personal appearance was as important to women then as it is now, and there were fashion trends in hairdressing. The Bob, the Shingle and the Eton Crop were all popular with younger women. The Eton Crop was more like a boy's style, but it particularly suited girls with good features. Older women often had Edwardian styles, done up on top, with a bun.

Perming was rather crude, with customers being "strung up" on machines. Then came the Maddison, where clamps were placed on the rolled hair and a timing device carefully set on the machine. An advancement was the Marcell Wave, which was an alternative to perming, and was done by using hot tongs. Colour shades were limited, but there was Innecto dyeing, Tunisian henna and bleaching. Conditioning was effected by massaging hot oils into the scalp. Hair was grown longer and worn longer. But perming could make the hair frizzy and many women did not like it. Twink perms came into being, which could be left on all night, and Toni and other cold perms, and as these innovations came onto the market the machines died out. Then, as now, tests had to be carried out on customers for allergic reactions.

Rates of pay were poor in the hairdressing trade, though much higher in London, of course, but then London salons required a diploma. It was customary to work on salary and

217

commission, each girl keeping her own tips. The presents we received at Christmas were always welcomed.'

EDITH INKSON

The Office Worker

'There was no scholarship in my time, and I left school at fourteen and went straight out to work, into sewing as a matter of fact, as a girl who lived nearby suggested I should try it. She actually gave me a coat to go in: we must have been hard-up!

Gladys Clayton & Co was the name of the firm I worked for and they made underclothes. This was in the basement of 62 Harpur Street. We did cutting out and machining. My boss liked my printing and asked if I would like to go into the office, and this I did. I used to do the wages for about thirty-two people. The site was later redeveloped and a lift was installed. The owners lived over the top of the premises.

I started working for this firm as a junior and finished up doing everything, typing, shorthand, ledgers, filing, doing the parcels up, taking them to the post, and going out with the boss delivering them. I went to St. Peter's Hall for private lessons in typewriting and shorthand, evening classes that is. These lessons were held in the rooms at the top. I had two typewriters in the office, a Remington which was a large typewriter, and a little tiny Corona portable. The staff were hourly-paid, and I had to use a Ready Reckoner to calculate payment. There was an ink duplicator in the office and I used to type the "skins" and do the duplicating. I was left in charge in later years when they went off to the seaside, and I looked after their dogs when they were away. Tom Clayton was the boss – it was just a husband and wife concern. She did the designing, and he was in charge of the office. She was the boss really! They were good friends to me and even came to my wedding. In fact they shut up shop and everybody came.

We used to have mannequin parades and all the literature

had to be sent out – the publicity. *Fashion parades these were.
Some girls came from London and some were our own girls.
We had china cups for drinks and somebody made little
sandwiches and cakes. It was a happy life. These fashion
parades were held at 64 Harpur Street or at Dudeney &
Johnsons in the High Street. We'd send out the notices, and
then book people in for the show. It was very hard work but
good for business. We had beautiful stuff, but I suppose
Rosamonds in Harpur Street were more elite than us, and
were really high-class tailors. We made a lot of children's
clothes. Some of the clients were quite wealthy but all sorts of
people came to the fashion parades.*

*My mother had worn very old-fashioned clothes, but many
of these were made by me. I took dress-making lessons at one
time. I also made clothes for my own children. I actually
learned the trade whilst working for this firm. We stocked a
wide range of materials, ribbons and laces. The window was
usually decorated with baby clothes and underwear,
camiknickers and French knickers made in silk.'*

WINIFRED BURTON

The Seamstress & Haberdasher

*'I was actually born in Canterbury, but lived in Bedford as a
young child with my parents Florence and Robert and my
younger brother Bob. My father served in the army in Egypt
and India, with the 10th Royal Hussars during the 1920s and
'30s, and we all went to live in India in the 1920s, returning
to England in 1935, when we moved to Luton.*

*It was exciting living in India at this time, and my mother
had a flair for, and enjoyed making, the splendid ballgowns
for the Officers' wives, and she took great delight in shopping
for beautiful materials and bargains from the rather dubious
bazaars which were really "out of bounds" to us. I can
remember going with her on our bicycles, and being
surrounded by throngs of staring people all straining to get a
look at us and jabbering away in their own tongue. You*

couldn't help feeling intimidated, frightened – I know I did – but my mother just kept going, as though she hadn't noticed. I thought she was very brave.

I went to boarding school up in the Himalayas for two years, where the weekly school sewing lesson, amongst other things, was making dreary uninspiring things such as navy school knickers! I did develop an interest in needlework, of course, because my mother was always dressmaking, and because some emphasis was placed on the subject at school. I was brought up to do sewing and knitting. I used to help my mother. She didn't advertise her services, but people in the regiment would ask her to make their clothes. She was properly apprenticed to dressmaking as a girl, in Bedford, and she told me she earned one shilling a week during that time. I was used to seeing her cutting up things, and altering and making clothes.

On returning to England, as a young woman, I met my husband and in 1948 we bought an established dressmaker's business called "Annes", in Biscot Road, Luton. The shop had been started by a person who was evacuated from London during the war, and she then returned to London after the war. It was empty when we bought it. I started out from scratch with £100 by making fancy aprons and things like that. During the war it was only possible to get £14-worth of wool per month. My husband didn't serve in the shop, but he did the book-work, and he made the wool racks, and we then stocked up with wools. Soon things began to blossom and I branched out into other handicrafts such as embroidery silks and linens, crochet cottons, materials, dressing table sets, shawls, rug-making materials and of course inevitably the wool and knitwear which proved to be the most popular of all.

Over the years I employed outworkers in order to cope with the volume of orders for the lovely Arran sweaters and cardigans, fine matinee sets for babies, school cardigans and so on. Requests for specially made knitwear came from as far afield as Australia, India, Ireland, and Canada, where the

*Irene pictured in the shop shortly after opening. She is wearing a
coat which she herself made, and which had a wine-velvet collar.*

*Arran jumpers especially are really appreciated. I even
supplied sweaters associated with such famous names as
John Wayne.*

*Today the sewing work is more in the nature of repairs and
alterations. The business has changed as demand has
changed, and now we sell to a lot of Asian people who do
sewing and make their own outfits. They are always buying
buttons, lace and ribbon, cottons, hairpins and things of that
nature. The one thing they don't seem to like doing is sewing
in zips, and I am often asked to do these.*

*I've been very busy over the years, and have come to know
many local people. We've had our moments: I can remember
sewing up a tea cosy in the back workroom for a waiting
customer who'd called in asking if we sold pom-pom hats.
Anything to oblige! On one occasion we had burglars, and
when I heard a disturbance upstairs I fortunately had the
presence of mind to lock the door at the bottom of the staircase*

A more recent picture of Irene's shop. In the window display is her granddaughter's Christening gown, and her grandmother's Singer treadle sewing machine, bought in 1925, and which her mother used, and subsequently gave to her.

and hurriedly went off for help. The news headlines read "Raiders stitched up"!

The shop has been my life, and I'm pleased to say that a great many of my regular customers have become life-long friends of mine.'

IRENE HORN

The Servant

The heyday of the domestic servant was truly during the Victorian era, but towards the end of the nineteenth century, life in domestic service was losing its appeal for many women, in preference to work in retailing, the manufacturing industries and clerical work. At the turn of the century the resident female domestic workforce is estimated to have been 1,330,783. The figure for men is estimated at 64,146.

A contributory factor in the demise of the domestic servant was the imposition of a tax on servants, [imposed in 1777 and abolished 1937: the tax on female servants imposed in 1785 was repealed in 1792 incidentally], compulsory education, the growth of industry and commerce, and the agricultural recession leading to a reduction in income for many landed families. However, it was not only land-owners who were forced to cut back on their domestic staff, but also many small traders and professional people, who also employed servants. Nevertheless, domestic service was still the largest employer of women in the country at the turn of the century, and this was the largest occupational group in the country.

'After I left school at fourteen I got a job living in with a family and looking after their little boy and girl. He was a gentleman farmer. His wife managed the household and ran the home and I cared for the two children. They had maids to do the work, of course. I had to bath the children at night and put them to bed, give them breakfast in the morning, take them out, keep them amused. I was paid half a crown a week for this.

Gentlemen farmers didn't rely on farming to provide a living and I think my employer had a private income in addition to his farming. They used to entertain a lot and had shoots. There was a cook, a kitchen maid, and one for the bedrooms. People were brought in from the village to help, when necessary. My employer had the first car I ever saw – a great big red one. The ladies wore flat hats with a veil tied under the chin, so they didn't blow off in the wind. These were Edwardian fashions of course, but practical.

This first job lasted for two years. I had my own room, which was better than most. The building was more modern than the average farm house. I ate with the children, not with the family. The children lived separately to their parents, but occasionally their mother would let them have tea with them, but they had very little to do with the children and might only see them once a day. The children didn't mind, they got to like the nannies better! The parents only took over when the children were older, more grown up, and went to university or finishing school. The little girl was sent to a finishing school in Florence when she got older. She had to be able to entertain and make a good marriage. The little boy seemed to like farming. He had a good education and probably took up farming himself. I think the father inherited most of the money, but the farm was a good hobby for him.

My next employer and his wife had just had their first baby. They kept a shop and needed someone to care for the child. Whilst I was with this family I had pneumonia and had to go into hospital.

My next employer was very rich, with a big mansion, grounds and statues. No title, but a big staff. I took care of their little boy and remained there for two and half years.

This couple were very kind to their staff, very friendly, and would always chat with you. They lived a very sociable life, left visiting cards at other people's homes, inviting them to visit. It was a Victorian life-style really. There was a big circle of friends and they used to give balls and different kinds of parties. They always dressed for dinner, which was quite formal. There was no resentment among the staff: we had never been used to anything else, other than what we had. I was on duty seven days a week and there were no paid holidays, but they gave us a holiday from time to time if we asked. They would get someone in from the village to take our place. We had about two hours off in the afternoon. The child's mother told me what to do, although they did have a housekeeper. I think they were happy times for everyone. We had to wear a uniform which was provided for us, a print dress. The print dresses were worn in the morning but in the afternoon and evening we had to wear black dresses with collars and cuffs. The print dress was like a working dress. I wore a tiny white apron, but the others wore large aprons that covered completely. If the staff were ill, they were put to bed and the doctor called in. Most of the staff lived in the attics but I lived with the children. The children had a school room where they could have first lessons. They went to boarding school when they were old enough, and then to Eton or one of those schools later on.'

MARY JEFFS

'I enjoyed my time in service at the farmhouse. It was a very varied life. We thought we were well above the station of the factory girls: we were taught things, and discipline. Factory girls didn't know how to do anything. No, I never regarded myself as inferior.'

WINIFRED ALLAN

'When I left school I went into service. It was only housework for girls, farms for boys. I went to the Midland Café in Midland Road at the top of Battleson Street, and worked from 7am to 6pm and to 8pm alternately. Every Saturday I had to work until 9pm and I got six shillings a week plus meals. They had one big room with single beds, and one other room, and took in commercials – representatives – for bed and breakfast, as well as serving coffee and meals which were cooked on a range. The cook was from Sawston in Cambridgeshire. I stayed there for about fifteen months then my mother died and my sister, who was looking after our dad, helped me to get into service.'

GWENDOLINE BROWN

'I left school the day I was fourteen, not staying on to the end of term, as was usual. My father couldn't afford to keep me at home so I went into service at Harlington Manor, working for Mrs Tabor, the lady of the manor, as a "between maid" – that is, between the housemaid and the cook. I did the washing up, made the beds, did the housework. Starting at 5am I got the range going, took cook up a cup of tea at 7am, got the staff's breakfast ready, laid the staff table and afterwards *cleared this table and washed up for both staff and the house. I finished work at 10pm, after scrubbing the kitchen floor. Fortunately for me the butler did the silver. For this I earned 6s 8d a week, plus meals, and lived in. Even for someone as accustomed to hard work as I was, the strain proved too much. I gave up and left after a month, to return home.'*

IVY FLUTE

'When I left school at fourteen, I wanted to be a teacher. My ambitions then changed, and I decided to go down the brick hill to work as the company had begun to employ women, but mother thought it was too rough and encouraged me to go into service. My school pal was Doll Ashpole. I can hear myself saying to mother "Doll Ashpole is working there, so why can't I go?" When we were at school I'd say "Doll Ashpole takes a h'penny to school, so why can't I?" and mother replied "She's got a father and you haven't, that's why". Doll lived at Keeley too, well it was known as Keeley Green then. She always seemed to have what I wanted, or to be able to do what I couldn't do.

My sister who was married and living at Mill Hill, helped me to get my first job. So I started as a between maid, helping all the maids, and then became a kitchen maid, and then progressed to being a parlour maid, until I got married. My employer, Mr Watson, was Managing Director of Studebaker Cars and Cadillacs and he often went to America. I was very surprised to see a friend of his called Cyril Mills, on "This Is Your Life" recently. Mr Mills was a frequent visitor to their home whilst I was there. The Mills family were something to do with Bertram Mills circus, and once a year all the staff were allowed to go to the circus for a special treat. Bertram Mills, Cyril's father, owned a farm at Edgware at that time. It was a good life there, but hard work mind you.

I had to wait on tables, clean the silver, valet the gentleman, brush his clothes and put his evening clothes out at night for him to dress for dinner; go and help the lady at *times to dress. They had two children, Nora and Douglas. I helped with the cooking and cleaned a great big stove with emery paper and cleaned the flue – hard work that was. All the food was prepared on a range. The staff had half a day off every week, and I often went to the pictures on these occasions, Golders Green Hippodrome, or went to my boyfriend's mother's. I started working there when I was fifteen and married at twenty-four and then left. My husband and I first set up home at Bushey Heath.'*   SARAH HILLS

'When I left school I first worked for Canon Briggs in Merton Road, Bedford, as a housemaid, and from there I moved to Shakespeare Road to work for a very well-known man and his family as Cook General. They had been in India, but he was a Director of a company in Tavistock Street, which manufactured cricket bats. In addition to cooking, I cleaned, took tea up to them in the evenings and when they had a whist drive, waited on them with drinks, etc. until about 10 o'clock at night. They would ring the bell for service. I had one afternoon off a week and one Sunday off in a fortnight, but I felt that they were very kind to me and I enjoyed working there.'   FREDA BROWN

'I worked as a cook general for a family with three children, who lived in Goldington Avenue, Bedford. This was about 1926, and the children's parents were in India. It was lovely, the best place I have ever been to. I did the cooking and housework and laid tables. The aunt who looked after the children helped out a lot. We worked together: she was a lovely person. There were two little girls and a boy who was seven then. I discovered, years later, that he was secretary of the Lovell Home Trust and a cricketer, playing for Bedfordshire. His son was also a cricketer for Bedfordshire. I lived in one of the Lovell properties for twelve years, until quite recently.'   GWENDOLINE BROWN

The Shop Assistant

'Having been made redundant at Cardington, I took a job at Woolworths in Bedford, where nothing was sold over the value of 6d. Hours of work were 9am to 7pm weekdays, 9am to 8pm Fridays and 9am to 9pm Saturdays. I cycled to work and back, a total distance of some twelve miles.

The first counter I was on at Woolworths sold gas equipment. Gas lights were used then – though not in Haynes village – and they stocked mantles and different things for gas.

I can still remember when Marks and Spencer had a bench in the old arcade, when they first started!'

BEATRICE 'MAY' WEBB

'I was paid a shilling a week for the first two years at Roses, where I ran errands, and worked in haberdashery, household linen and dress materials. There was a good selection of ready-made clothes to be had then but many women made their own clothes. During slack times wages were cut and short-time working introduced. The apprentices were expected to dress neatly and to tie their hair back with a black bow.

My next job was at the Dorothy Guppy shop, where I earned five shillings per week working as an "improver". This millinery shop was also in St. Peter's Street, Bedford.'

HILDA HAYDEN

'My sister Winnie did an apprenticeship at E P Rose's, High Street, Bedford, in the Glove Department. The apprentices were sent away for training, to learn about different skins and about management of the department. You would do four years then before you actually sold a glove. The training was very thorough. Winnie lived in at Rose's annexe in De Parys Avenue. She started on five shillings a week the first year and by her fourth year she was earning one pound a week.

Rose's was the place to shop in Bedford then. They sold a wide range of goods, haberdashery and many other things, as Debenhams do today. The men wore morning frocks and tails and there were floor walkers who opened the door for you. Other popular shops with women were Dusts, an old-fashioned but classy shop, and Kate Owens. These both sold ladies' gowns.'

EDITH INKSON

CONTRIBUTORS

WINIFRED LOUISA ALLAN (NÉE HODBY)

Winnie was born at Knotting Green on 8 January 1919. Her father and his father were also born there, in a tied cottage near the church. Her father spent all his working life on Green Farm, owned by Mr Pike. There were no privately owned properties in the village at that time. Of the six children born to Winnie's parents, one died at the age of twelve with appendicitis.

Winnie's family have always been active church members. Her grandfather was an organist and her father too, both self-taught. One vicar (Rev. Wiggins) looked after two parishes then, Knotting and Souldrop. Most village people were church-goers and at harvest festival and the Knotting Feast the church would be packed to capacity.

Winnie met her husband in Bedford in 1938. He was in the Airforce training at Cardington, but he came from Scotland. He was posted to Mildenhall but they kept in touch and were married on New Year's Eve, 1941. As a time-serving airman, he saw action in the Second World War, and was invalided out in 1944.

ERIC GEORGE BALDOCK

Eric was born on 24 March 1909 in Dunstable. His father worked as a Engineer/Turner at SKF Co and his mother worked at home, straw plaiting for the hat trade. The town was full of hat making firms when he was young.

There were five children in Eric's family, two boys and three girls. One of his sisters who lived in one of the Almshouses in Church Street, was a teacher turned missionary, who spent twenty years in Lahore and other areas of Pakistan. Their parents were both church-goers and his father was a member of the choir. Eric and his wife were both Sunday School teachers at the Priory church.

RICHARD BARROWS

Richard, (always known as 'Dick'), was born in London's East End on 28 June 1909. One of eight children, his father was a shoe-maker. He has lived in Sandy since 1933. He and his late wife had four children, Edith, Richard, Jean and Alan, and there are eleven grandchildren. His main interest has been dancing and this is a hobby which his son Alan took up for several years. They have belonged to various clubs, and danced at many company dances over the years. He retired sixteen years ago, at the age of seventy, and now enjoys TV, wireless and gardening. He has never smoked and is a teetotaller.

EDMUND CHARLES BOURNE

Edmund was born in December 1882. He moved to Dunstable from Plumstead in 1919 and started a grocer's shop in High Street North, with his twin brother. Some time after his brother's return to London, the name of the business was changed from Bourne Bros to E C Bourne. Edmund regularly attended the Methodist Church, The Square, where he was regarded with high esteem and where he held a number of senior positions.

MAURICE CHARLES BOYLES

Maurice was born in Marston on 7 October 1928 at his maternal grandmother's home. The family moved to Wootton where he attended Wootton School until the age of fourteen, and remained in Wootton until his marriage at the age of twenty-four to a girl from Cranfield. He worked for his father after leaving school, and took over the business when his father retired in 1968. After his marriage he moved to Cranfield and has lived in the same house since 1955. He hopes to remain there for the rest of his days.

FREDA ELIZABETH BROWN (NÉE COOKE)

Freda was born on 15 April 1914, at 53 Russell Street, Bedford, the eldest of five children. Her father was in the 11th and 13th Hussars, and he married her mother in 1910.

Freda's parents were both Bedfordians, and her father worked at the gas works in Queens Park for most of his life, but there were times when he was out of work, and her mother then went out waitressing at the County Club near the Swan Hotel.

GWENDOLINE ELSIE BROWN (NÉE JEFFRIES)

Gwen was born in Clapham on 16 June 1908. Her father was a gardener and gravedigger and for ten years of his life he worked solely as a gravedigger at Bedford Cemetery. Gwen's parents had twelve children, of whom nine survived. Four of her brothers were in the first world war.

Gwen met her husband whilst in service at Sharnbrook, and married at the age of twenty. They had seven children. He was a farm worker having worked for some years at Samuel Whitbread's farm near Shefford, and also at Hill Farm, Chellington, but ill health forced him to leave the farm and he then got a job with the Ministry at Twinwoods (from where Glen Miller took off on his last fated flight).

Gwen's husband died in 1968.

FREDERICK BURRAWAY

Fred, one of seven children, was born in 1905 in a cottage in Cause End Road, Wootton, which has since been demolished. His father worked as a Setter for the London Brick Company, then known as Forders Ltd. Fred has lived all his life in the village and has many memories of Wootton and its people, since his early days.

After a two-year courtship, Fred married his wife at the age of twenty-two and took a cottage near the bakehouse where he worked all his life. He has very happy memories of a lifetime spent in the employ of the Juffs family, local bakers, and maintains that given the opportunity he would love to do it all over again.

WINIFRED BURTON (NÉE POULTER)

Winnie was born on 1 October 1909 in Cricket Lane, Bedford, in a thatched cottage which has since disappeared. Her parents moved to School Yard when she was about three, at the back of Barkers Lane and near to Goldington School. Winnie's father was a sheet metal worker at Allens, as was his father. There were three children in the family.

Winnie was married at twenty-four, to a painter, decorator and signwriter, and continued to work only as a holiday relief, until her son was born.

FRANK PERCY CHAPMAN

Frank was born on 3 March 1900 at 31 Ashton Street, Luton, where he lived until he was married at twenty-three. His mother didn't want him to have a motor for the wedding, so he had to get a carriage and pair of greys. Powdrill did the wedding (they were building contractors and had a farm) and as Frank lived only two minutes from the church, they were driven right round the town before actually going into church. Rudds, where his mother worked, did the wedding cake, for which they charged two pounds: Frank thought it was worth five at least! He regarded this as a favour, since they were friends and neighbours.

On the occasion of his Diamond Wedding Anniversary, Frank and his wife received a telegram from the Queen, of which he is very proud.

CHRISTOPHER JOHN CREAMER

Chris was born on 14 December 1903 at Church End, Milton Bryan. His father was a woodman/forester on the Woburn Estate. Their home was a charity cottage, belonging to the Milton Bryan Charity. Chris's grandfather, Levi Creamer, worked on Manor Farm, which was part of the Battlesden Estate. His mother played the organ at the local church from the time she was nine years old, and her mother – grandmother Clark – who had always lived in Milton Bryan, died at the age of 97.

Chris officially retired at 65, but received no pension, and has worked since then for a local farmer, hedging and ditching, and helping with the cows.

WILFRED DENNIS

Wilfred was born at Ruxox Farm in Flitwick, where his father was a tenant farmer, on 8 October 1928. He was a pupil at Greenfield School, and after leaving school and a brief period working for a baker in Clophill, went on to cultivate and sell produce as a travelling greengrocer. Wilfred and his wife married in 1964 and have one daughter, who went to Oxford University and is now a teacher. Now retired, he is still busy with his garden, greenhouse and two allotments, and is an active and committed Methodist preacher.

IVY FLUTE (NÉE LAWSON)

Ivy was born on 16 February 1916 at Radwell, a hamlet near Felmersham. Her father was the local rag-and-bone merchant, known as 'Raggy Lawson'.

Ivy's father collapsed and died after a trip to London, in 1950, aged 72. Ivy inherited enough money to send her son to Bedford Modern School and he went on to university and is now a teacher. She remembers her father with admiration and affection.

HILDA HAYDEN

Hilda was born in St. Cuthbert, Bedford, on Boxing Day of 1894, and was the last of eleven children. Her father had his own decorating business, and she thinks the family were comfortably-off. The large house in Newnham Street where she grew up, had four bedrooms with two large reception rooms downstairs and a lobby.

During Hilda's courting days she and her sisters were only allowed to take boyfriends home when they had decided if they 'wanted them'. One of her friends became pregnant, and she and her sisters Alice and Connie were told quite bluntly that if anything like that happened to them, father would not have them in the house. She was twenty-nine when she married, but she was a good girl!

TERENCE BRIAN HEADEY

Terence was born on 30 March 1930 at Westleigh, West Street, Dunstable, at his grandparents' home (he is

a fifth generation Dunstablian). The house is now occupied by Mr Robert Gutteridge, solicitor, a member of another old Dunstable family. Terence was educated at Dunstable Grammar School and left in 1945 to join the family business of Nurserymen and Florists. He took charge of the business at the age of twenty, when his father died, and retired after fifty years in the business. He is married, and he and Prudence, his wife, have three children, and two grandchildren. His interests are Grand Prix Racing, as a spectator, walking, his dogs, the countryside and study of nature. He now lives in a delightful cottage in the middle of Ashridge, in 'total happiness'.

SARAH ANN HILLS (NÉE LOWE)

Sarah was born on 3 October 1900 in Cause End Road, Wootton,

next door to the shop and the Star Public House. This property has since been demolished. Her grandmother's home was one of the four Yeoman's Cottages at Chennell's Farm, then owned by Mr Frossell, and it was from there that her mother moved to Cause End Road to live following her marriage. When Sarah was a year old her parents moved to Keeley, Wootton. Both parents were from Wootton, and father was a thatcher by trade. Sarah was only three years old when he died of pneumonia, leaving her mother to raise four children, Sarah being the youngest.

MABEL DORIS HILLYARD (NÉE STANTON)

Mabel was born on 12 December 1913 in Priory Street, Bedford. She had one brother. Her father, Walter Stanton, was a blacksmith. He traded in Commercial Road, where the Council works were. He was actually employed by the Corporation and did all the ironwork for Bedford, all the fancy gates. He was in the army during the First World War and during this time her mother often went out scrubbing floors. He suffered from dysentry whilst in the forces, and his weight reduced to six stone at one time, but he survived the war and returned to his smithy, where he worked for forty-eight years in all.

IRENE HORN (NÉE DAY)

Irene was born on 17 May 1920 in Canterbury, Kent. Her father served with the British army in Egypt and India and she lived abroad with her parents until the age of fifteen, when the family returned to England. Her father was then employed at the Post Office and lived to be ninety-five: her mother died in 1944 at the age of forty-six. Irene and her husband Stuart had one daughter, Janet, and a son, Martin, and her husband and daughter have assisted with her business in Biscot Road, Luton, which she has operated now for forty-six years.

EDITH INKSON (NÉE COLLINS)

Edith was born in Northamptonshire on 28 October 1910, and came to live with her spinster aunt at Bury End, which was about a mile and a half from Stagsden, when she was twelve, following the death of her parents. Her father was killed when he was thrown from a pony and trap in Rushden, where he was in business manufacturing shoes, and her mother died of pernicious anaemia.

There were seven children in the family, but the eldest boy died of meningitis, leaving three boys and three girls, two of whom were twins (Edith and Grace).

MARY JEFFS (NÉE COOLING)

Mary was born on 26 December 1893 in West Bromwich, Staffordshire, and came to Bedford in the 1920s to stay with an aunt who was living in Kempston. She only came for a holiday, but loved the place so much that she decided to stay. West Bromwich was the Black Country, all coal mines, and Bedford seemed a complete change, to her.

Mary's mother died at the age of twenty-five, when Mary was a young child, and she was raised by her father's mother in Warwickshire. She thinks her father worked in the iron foundries but is not sure. He was in the First World War and returned, but didn't live long afterwards. She was his only child.

Mary's grandfather was a farm worker. Her grandparents' home was in Butlers Marston, just a little hamlet about nine miles from Stratford-on-Avon. This was hunting country, and the local hunt was the Warwickshire hounds. Lord Willoughby de Broke had a large country estate there: he did a lot of private work for the Queen Mother.

WILLIAM ALAN JORDAN

John, as he has always been known, was born at Sandy Mill, 2 St. Neots Road, on 29 November 1920. A very energetic and industrious man, he has for many years been the driving force behind the milling business known as W Jordan and Sons. At the age of seventy-one, he works full-time and still finds time to pursue his life-long interests in flying and motor racing. He was associated with the Shuttleworth Trust for twenty-three years, flying their aircraft and testing on their behalf, and now flies his Boeing Steerman which 'loops from take-off' as an aerobatic and stunt pilot. He frequently races at Silverstone, Snetterton, etc., in his Lola T330.

Fit and sufficiently agile as to be the envy of men far younger, he sprints from place to place and runs up the steep and narrow flights of stairs between the three floors of the mill, rapidly descending backwards ship-style, in no less an impressive fashion. A veritable power-house of energy!

ERNEST LAIN

Ernest was born on 28 April 1903 in Hurst Grove, Queens Park, Bedford, where Allens' works and offices are now situated. His father was a commercial traveller in chemists' sundries. He never wasted anything, and the samples often went into the bath on Saturday night. There was always a dose of something to be had – even Epsom Salts!

Ernest's thwarted ambition was to be a concert pianist, but he has played and enjoyed piano all his life, and still plays every day. He was married in 1930 to a girl who has been the only love of his life. Sadly, she passed away in 1968. Their son Tony, and his wife, have 'been marvellous', and Ernest has three lovely grandchildren, four great-grandchildren and another is due in June.

STANLEY GEORGE LOVELL

Stan was born on 9 March 1909 in Hall End, Wootton. He was one of three chldren, and his father was a general labourer – a bricklayer's labourer – who worked at the brickworks, and for Samuel Foster, the builders in Kempston, where Bushbys are now situated. He also worked for Mr Lunnis, the builder at 'Tags End' which is now called Cause End Road. After leaving school at fourteen, Stan worked at the local brickworks for many years.

Stan was in the St. John's Ambulance Brigade for twenty-five years, at Stewartby and then at Kempston, and only left the Brigade in 1954, when he was diagnosed as having a brain tumour. He received medical training in Sidmouth, Devon and was a male nurse with the RAF at Weeton near Blackpool and then at North Allerton, until he was demobbed. He helped to set it up, in North Allerton, and was there when the first patient arrived. It was like a general hospital for the Air Force. He chose this career course with the RAF because of his experience in the St. John's Ambulance Brigade.

ETHEL ANNIE MAYES (NÉE JARVIS)

Ethel was born in Luton on 30 August 1899. Her mother died when she was three, and, left with a family of six children, her father re-married. His second wife had been employed as a housekeeper in a big house. She looked after Annie and brought her up well: 'she was a very good person'. There were no children from this second marriage.

Ethel's husband had always worked for his uncle, who had a shop in Hastings Street (now the site of a block of offices) called Rumblows. They did watch and clock repairs. The uncle had no children and when he died he left the business to Ethel's husband. She and her two sons continued to run it for quite some time after the death of her husband. It was well-known locally.

FREDERICK MOORE

Fred was born on 11 February 1913 at No. 271 High Street North, Dunstable (later changed to No. 112), over the original shop which his parents Alice and Charles acquired in 1908 and which was situated near the corner of George Street. Having attended Dunstable School, Fred left at the age of sixteen and after being articled in Luton, qualified as a Chartered Accountant. After some years in accountancy, he came into the family business on the illness of his parents, and loved it so much he stayed. He was joined in the business by his wife and subsequently by his daughter Pauline. The business is still a private partnership.

Fred has always been involved in the Methodist Church and the Circuit of which it is the head, as were his parents and three brothers. He is still Church Treasurer, an office he has held for over thirty years. He has also taken services in the Circuit as a Local Preacher.

Now in retirement, Fred's leisure activities include gardening, golf and music.

RONALD EDWARD OVERHILL

Ron was born on 8 August 1915 at Lyndhurst Road, Luton. He had one brother and his father was a hat block maker by trade and later a local councillor and keen Freemason. Both his parents lived to a good age, his mother being ninety-nine when she passed away in 1990. Ron started in the hat trade straight from Luton Modern School and eventually owned his own hat factory in Luton. In the war he was a cypher officer in the RAF and has been married for fifty-five years. His life-long hobby has been golf which he still plays today.

EDWARD JOHN PAGE

Ted was born at 10 Dane Street, Bedford, where the Bedford Post Office is now situated, on 30 May 1907. His parents died when he was sixteen, and Ted was left to take care of his younger brother and sister. He left school at thirteen and started work as a blacksmith in Dane Street. He has worked as a blacksmith all his life and reckons he has always had a good life.

WALTER REGINALD PARROTT

Walter, who has always been known as Reg, was born on 28 January 1901 in a stone and thatched cottage in the village of Milton Ernest.

Reg married in 1927 and set up home in Thurleigh. In 1959 he and his wife acquired a sixteen acre smallholding in Keysoe and planned to grow wheat crops and to use the straw for thatching. Despite the untimely death of his wife in 1963 at the age of 57, he carried on, but after retirement, returned to live in Milton Ernest in a little cottage overlooking the park where he had spent many happy hours in his younger days watching cricket. 'Living by myself was not my way of life, being one of a large family and a family man myself' (Reg was one of eleven children, and he and his wife had four children).

Subsequently Reg re-married, his new wife having been a neighbour and friend of long-standing. They lived in a stone and thatched cottage in Thurleigh Road, Milton Ernest, similar in many respects to the cottage in which Reg was born. From his cottage home he could see the church to the left, and on the right, on Church Green, the school, both of which he attended in his young days.

WILLIAM GEORGE FRANK PERRIDGE

Frank, as he has always been known, was born on 20 November 1901 in Southhill, on Mr Samuel Whitbread's estate where the sawmills were run by his father, George, who originated in Silverstone, Northamptonshire. Frank left school when the war started, and after a couple of years on the farm, began work in the timber trade. During his time on the farm, there were only old men and boys available for work. He enjoyed working with horses, and helping with ploughing. For many years Frank worked with his father, who died in 1943. He has spent the remainder of his working life in the timber trade.

ARTHUR THOMAS SEDGEWICK

Arthur was born on 8 April 1922 in Aspley Guise. His father worked on various farms, and his mother also worked on the land for quite a few years. He met his wife at Aspley Heath, where she worked as an auxiliary nurse at Dayswood Nursing Home. The Home was surrounded by connifers, the smell of which was considered beneficial for sufferers of TB and chest ailments. After forty-six years on the Bedford Estate, Arthur retired through ill-health in 1963. He still enjoys shooting and is a member of the Shefford and District Shooting Club. He is a member of the Royal Agricultural Society and has a medal presented to him for forty years of work on the estate. He still occupies his estate house at Ridgemont which is his to occupy for the remainder of his life.

PERCIVAL GEOFFREY SHERWOOD

'Geoff' was born at 17 Battison Street, Bedford on 27 May 1919. Owing to the fact that his father's brother was also called Percival, he was always known as Geoff, and still is. His father was an electrical engineer, and his father before him was a blacksmith engineer on the Railway. After leaving Queen's Park School in 1934, he was employed at the Igranic Company in Bedford from 1934 to 1942, when he was conscripted, but returned to his employer and was then engaged on priority work for the war effort. After other assignments, he returned to the Igranic in 1946. He was Chief Fire Officer of the Igranic Fire Brigade from 1950 until 1968, when it was disbanded, a member of the Works First Aid Party, and also a member of the Civil Defence Rescue Team and held a 'Gold Star' Civil Defence Rescue Instructor's Certificate. He was also a member of the Bedfordshire Ambulance Team. It was not until 1970 that he took responsibility for his father's antiques business, but he has always been connected with it. His hobbies over the years have included bowls, darts, skittles, fishing and gardening.

ARTHUR 'LOL' LAWRENCE THEW

'Lol', as he was always known, was born on 31 October 1903 in the end one of three cottages in Harrold High Street, which stood opposite the present garage. There were three children in the family, and his father worked in the leather trade. His grandfather was a shepherd.

After leaving school at 13, Lol wanted to join the airforce, which he could not do until the age of fifteen. He did get as far as London in an attempt to join up, but failed because of his poor eyesight. He also wanted to go to Australia, but could not because his mother would not consent. He subsequently joined his father in the leather industry.

ERIC THORNE

Eric was born on 9 January 1896 in Woburn and was the third child of five. His father owned a butcher's shop in High Street North, Dunstable, at one time, and was always connected with farming and animals.

In 1921 Eric and his brother Cyril sailed to Australia. It was a very hard life and they had to do odd jobs to earn a living. They slept rough many times, not having sufficient money to pay for lodgings. At one time Eric rode a horse in a race and also entered the boxing ring as a contestant, to make money. Cyril met a girl and settled down, but although Eric was not afraid of hard work, he gave up and came home after two years. A year later he married Maude Durante of Houghton Road and settled down in Markyate where their son Frank was born. In 1930 he bought a piece of land in Beale Street from his father and had a house built, in which he lived until his death in 1985.

BEATRICE MAY WEBB (NÉE JEFFORD)

May, as she has always been known, was born in Hounslow, Middlesex, on 28 July 1906. Her father was Haynes born, and this is where all of his family lived. At the time May was born, he was working as a builder's labourer – a yard-man – in Chiswick, and when he was drafted into the army in 1914, her mother moved back to Haynes to be near his family. May's mother was born in Wiltshire, but had been in service in Hounslow before their marriage.

May's father was killed in action on 4 November 1918, a few days before the armistice was signed.

May's husband's family came from near Biggleswade, where his father was a smallholder. He and his parents moved to May's present cottage home in 1919, and they married in 1933. Her mother-in-law was an independent lady who worked on the land and continued to do so until she was in her seventies, at which time she qualified for a pension. May's husband was a farm worker all his life.

FREDERICK WALLACE WILDMAN

Fred was born on 27 August 1893 at 1 Cross End, Thurleigh. He was the eldest of seven children and was born in the house in which his grandmother was born and where his parents set up home when they married. Fred's father was a carpenter, wheelwright and undertaker. Fred worked for his father before leaving school, and after leaving school at twelve. In later life he was a very energetic member of his community – in particular within the Church, the Cricket Club, in fund-raising and so on.

Fred lived an active and long life, and enjoyed good health. At the age of ninety-four he was breaking bricks to lay a new driveway!

ALEC WILFRID WILMOT

Alec was born on 29 March 1913 in Southill and has worked all his life as a piano tuner/repairer. He married in 1939 and had one daughter Sandra, who has been very supportive.

He and his wife Gwen have shared many interests including cycling, dancing, walking, and camping. He regularly attends Yoga, enjoys 'keep fit', aerobics and swimming. Since losing his wife three years ago, he has been an active supporter of various charitable causes, and has established the Gwen Wilmot Alzheimer's Memorial Fund, to which he contributes money each year on the anniversary of her death from Alzheimer's Disease.

BEATRICE MAY WOODWARD (NÉE PALMER)

Beatrice's parents met in Sandy, where her mother was a private nurse and her father coachman to an elderly gentleman who was the author of the book *Ampthill Towers*. They married and moved to Maulden, and this is where she was born on 4 September 1901, at Green End. Her father was then employed as a farm worker.

There were nine children in the family, and they occupied two of the Duke of Bedford's cottages which were made into one. Most of the farms in the area were then tenanted, and owned by the Duke.

Beatrice married in 1927 and she and her husband became market gardeners in Maulden.

Index to Locations

Books Published by
THE BOOK CASTLE

JOURNEYS INTO HERTFORDSHIRE: Anthony Mackay.
Foreword by The Marquess of Salisbury, Hatfield House.
Nearly 200 superbly detailed ink drawings depict the towns, buildings
and landscape of this still predominantly rural county.

JOURNEYS INTO BEDFORDSHIRE: Anthony Mackay.
Foreword by The Marquess of Tavistock, Woburn Abbey.
A lavish book of over 150 evocative ink drawings.

CHILTERN ARCHAEOLOGY: RECENT WORK:
A Handbook for the Next Decade: edited by Robin Holgate.
The latest views, results and excavations by twenty-three leading
archaeologists throughout the Chilterns.

COUNTRYSIDE CYCLING IN BEDFORDSHIRE,
BUCKINGHAMSHIRE AND HERTFORDSHIRE: Mick Payne.
Twenty rides on- and off-road for all the family.

LOCAL WALKS: South Bedfordshire and North Chilterns:
Vaughan Basham. Twenty-seven thematic circular walks.

LOCAL WALKS : North and Mid-Bedfordshire: Vaughan Basham.
Twenty-five thematic circular walks.

CHILTERN WALKS: Hertfordshire, Bedfordshire and
North Buckinghamshire: Nick Moon.

CHILTERN WALKS: Buckinghamshire: Nick Moon.

CHILTERN WALKS: Oxfordshire and West Buckinghamshire:
Nick Moon. A trilogy of circular walks, in association with the
Chiltern Society. Each volume contains thirty circular walks.

OXFORDSHIRE WALKS: Oxford, the Cotswolds and
the Cherwell Valley: Nick Moon.

OXFORDSHIRE WALKS: Oxford, the Downs and
the Thames Valley: Nick Moon.
Two volumes that complement Chiltern Walks: Oxfordshire and
complete coverage of the county, in association with the Oxford
Fieldpaths Society. Thirty circular walks in each.

FOLK: Characters and Events in the History of Bedfordshire and Northamptonshire: Vivienne Evans. Anthology about people of yesteryear – arranged alphabetically by village or town.

LEGACIES: Tales and Legends of Luton and the North Chilterns: Vic Lea. Twenty-five mysteries and stories based on fact, including Luton Town Football Club. Many photographs.

ECHOES: Tales And Legends of Bedfordshire and Hertfordshire: Vic Lea. Thirty, compulsively retold historical incidents.

MYTHS and WITCHES, PEOPLE and POLITICS:
Tales from Four Shires: Bucks., Beds., Herts., and Northants.: John Houghton.
Anthology of strange but true historical events.

ECCENTRICS and VILLAINS, HAUNTINGS and HEROES.:
Tales from Four Shires: Northants., Beds., Bucks. and Herts.: John Houghton.
True incidents and curious events covering one thousand years.

THE RAILWAY AGE IN BEDFORDSHIRE: Fred Cockman.
Classic, illustrated account of early railway history.

JOHN BUNYAN: HIS LIFE AND TIMES: Vivienne Evans.
Foreword by the Bishop of Bedford. Preface by Terry Waite.
Bedfordshire's most famous son set in his seventeenth century context.

SWANS IN MY KITCHEN: The Story of a Swan Sanctuary:
Lis Dorer. Foreword by Dr Philip Burton. Updated edition.
Tales of her dedication to the survival of these beautiful birds through her sanctuary near Hemel Hempstead.

WHIPSNADE WILD ANIMAL PARK: 'MY AFRICA': Lucy Pendar.
Foreword by Andrew Forbes. Introduction by Gerald Durrell.
Inside story of sixty years of the Park's animals and people – full of anecdotes, photographs and drawings.

DUNSTABLE WITH THE PRIORY, 1100–1550: Vivienne Evans.
Dramatic growth of Henry I's important new town around a major crossroads.

DUNSTABLE DECADE: THE EIGHTIES: –
A Collection of Photographs: Pat Lovering.
A souvenir book of nearly 300 pictures of people and events in the 1980s.

DUNSTABLE IN DETAIL: Nigel Benson.
A hundred of the town's buildings and features, plus town trail map.

OLD DUNSTABLE: Bill Twaddle.
A new edition of this collection of early photographs.

BOURNE AND BRED: A Dunstable Boyhood Between the Wars:
Colin Bourne.
An elegantly written, well-illustrated book capturing the spirit of the town over fifty years ago.

ROYAL HOUGHTON: Pat Lovering.
Illustrated history of Houghton Regis from the earliest times to the present.

BEDFORDSHIRE'S YESTERYEARS Vol. 1:
The Family, Childhood and Schooldays: Brenda Fraser-Newstead.
Unusual early 20th century reminiscences, with private photographs.

BEDFORDSHIRE'S YESTERYEARS Vol 2:
The Rural Scene: Brenda Fraser-Newstead.
Vivid first-hand accounts of country life two or three generations ago.

BEDFORDSHIRE'S YESTERYEARS Vol 3:
Craftsmen and Trades People: Brenda Fraser-Newstead.
Fascinating recollections over several generations practising many vanishing crafts and trades.

PUBS and PINTS:
The Story of Luton's Public Houses and Breweries: Stuart Smith.
Three hundred rare photographs illustrate this detailed account of the town's important brewing industry and retail beer outlets, past and present.

THE CHANGING FACE OF LUTON: An Illustrated History:
Stephen Bunker, Robin Holgate and Marian Nichols.
Luton's development from earliest times to the present busy industrial town. Illustrated in colour and monochrome. The three authors from Luton Museum are all experts in local history, archaeology, crafts and social history.

THE MEN WHO WORE STRAW HELMETS:
Policing Luton, 1840–1974: Tom Madigan.
Meticulously chronicled history; dozens of rare photographs; author served Luton Police for nearly fifty years.

BETWEEN THE HILLS:
The Story of Lilley, a Chiltern Village: Roy Pinnock.
A priceless piece of our heritage – the rural beauty remains but the customs and way of life described here have largely disappeared.

GLEANINGS REVISITED:
Nostalgic Thoughts of a Bedfordshire Farmer's Boy: E W O'Dell.
His own sketches and early photographs adorn this lively account of rural Bedfordshire in days gone by.

FARM OF MY CHILDHOOD, 1925–1947: Mary Roberts.
An almost vanished lifestyle on a remote farm near Flitwick.

THE TALL HITCHIN SERGEANT:
A Victorian Crime Novel based on fact: Edgar Newman.
Mixes real police officers and authentic background with an exciting storyline.

THE TALL HITCHIN INSPECTOR'S CASEBOOK: A Victorian Crime Novel based on fact: Edgar Newman.
Worthies of the time encounter more archetypal villains.

LEAFING THROUGH LITERATURE:
Writers' Lives in Hertfordshire and Bedfordshire: David Carroll.
Illustrated short biographies of many famous authors and their connections with these counties.

THROUGH VISITORS' EYES: A Bedfordshire Anthology:
edited by Simon Houfe.
Impressions of the county by famous visitors over the last four centuries, thematically arranged and illustrated with line drawings.

THE HILL OF THE MARTYR:
An Architectural History of St. Albans Abbey: Eileen Roberts.
Scholarly and readable chronological narrative history of Hertfordshire and Bedfordshire's famous cathedral. Fully illustrated with photographs and plans.

SPECIALLY FOR CHILDREN

VILLA BELOW THE KNOLLS: A Story of Roman Britain:
Michael Dundrow.
An exciting adventure for young John in Totternhoe and Dunstable two thousand years ago.

ADVENTURE ON THE KNOLLS: A Story of Iron Age Britain:
Michael Dundrow.
Excitement on Totternhoe Knolls as ten-year-old John finds himself back in those dangerous times, confronting Julius Caesar and his army.

THE RAVENS: One Boy Against the Might of Rome: James Dyer.
On the Barton Hills and in the south-east of England as the men of the great fort of Ravensburgh (near Hexton) confront the invaders.

Further titles are in preparation.
All the above are available via any bookshop, or from the publisher and bookseller
THE BOOK CASTLE
12 Church Street, Dunstable, Bedfordshire, LU5 4RU
Tel: (01582) 605670